A
THEORY OF
HUMANITY: A LOVE STORY

An Instruction Manual
on How to Live
in Higher Vibrations

Written through the hands of
Ale

with Support and Contributions from
Tamara Elbl Newman

www.atheoryofhumanity.com
www.freespiritway.com

Design
Beatriz Burecovics

TABLE OF CONTENTS

A FEW WORDS FROM

ALE

I am Human and everything that signifies. I know who I am. This instruction manual was written through my hands, it wasn't solely from me. It came from love. With this, my intention is to allow ourselves to surf the wave crest of the Vibration of Love, and to make the lulls between the waves, our insecurities, be so superficial that they no longer affect us emotionally. That is who Ale is: it is when I am surfing the wave of love with the intention of love, receiving (and just as important) accepting the love, and this manual was written in that vibration. The way I want to do this is through explanation and with that open discussion, possibilities, and advances for us all.

Throughout this book, because of the subjects discussed, there is a possibility that we will fall into a lull of insecurities through being pensive about this theory and how it possibly correlates to those insecurities. This is going from the crest to a lull. This is natural and is what needs to be healed, ergo the reason for the book. We live in cycles, which can be positive or negative, and, at the same time, there are moments of decision and action in our lives that change the gears to another cycle, which can also be positive or negative. My intention is to give reference to how to change the gear to a positive cycle and to forever be able to surf the wave of love and at the same time have your lull feel as soft as the foam the wave makes when meeting the sand.

TAMARA

I feel an excitement about what is coming next for Humanity as we begin to become aware of the beautiful beings that we are. I am so grateful to understand what I understand about our Truth and the amazing possibilities that we can create together as we begin to trust each other and ourselves, letting go of past beliefs of who we are or who we have been. I believe that when we realize our Truth and why we are here and accept the reality of our purpose as a collective as well as individuals, we will begin to embark on a new experience of ourselves where everyone thrives and lives their best life. This book is part of the beginning of the movement towards falling in love with ourselves. As we understand more the reasons for past suffering and pain, we can collectively mourn and forgive what we have gone through so we can be free of the past and transform it. By acknowledging and respecting our current comprehension which supports everyone in the transition from the old programming of the past negative perspective of our Humanity to a new experience of ourselves in the future, the Universe is becoming more through us and our important role in the expansion of all.

DEDICATION

TAMARA

To Humanity: May you bow humbly to yourself for your
willingness of allowing the possibility of forgetting the
Truth of Who you are
to come back into this experience of contrast in order to heal
it, so that All Beings in existence may experience

Eternal Life and Love to its *fullest.*

This is dedicated to *Ale*

every conscious Light

every Energy

Love

Mantra Reference Page

The theory proposes that we are energy and live in emotional waves. This instruction manual might cause movement in our emotional waves. Everything can cause these movements, called *lulls*, depending on the experience. This reference page is not only if you do fall into the lull of the wave while reading this but also for other aspects of emotional understanding. To be able to read the instruction manual and to integrate it, we want to begin by inviting you to learn your *Mantra*.

What is the *Mantra?*

The Mantra is your Loving Inspirational Truth Energy (LITE). Your Mantra is your LITE. Your Mantra is your light. The Mantra is a beautiful loving truth about yourself, about life, and can be felt emotionally when you repeat it to yourself. The Mantra is a word or phrase that you can use in order to raise your emotional vibration when you fall into a lull. It works in every moment of your emotional wave of life because it is your LITE in every vibration. This LITE about you will lift yourself from the lull of the wave and will help you change your wave pattern. It can be accessed at any time and with practice will work on its own to help you recognize when you are going into negative energy. It is the love that we are that we are celebrating with the Mantra. It will remind us of who we really are and how we share that truth with others and experience that truth through others. The Mantra, though it seems simple, is actually complex in its abilities. The Mantra is an energetic grappling hook to help us get to higher vibrations, it can help limit the amount of negative energy we feel, it is always there to emotionally support us, it can help us with our wave patterns to get out of cycles, and **the LITE is Us reminding Ourselves who We are**.

WHY USE THE *MANTRA?*

We are energy and when we dance and connect in the positive and negative it makes no difference, but **when we are energy and Human we emotionally feel when we harmonize with vibrations** which has been a confusion throughout the history of Humanity. When we find ourselves in the negative part of the wave, we feel negative emotions and thoughts, and in this insecurity, there is a possibil-ity of feeling lost emotionally. We might make decisions in this insecurity that can have distortions that don't benefit us in the long term but help in the short term to get out of the negative energy. We didn't understand that we, as energy, were looking for a vibration to harmonize with and feel, even in the negative. We have done this because we didn't really understand that there were other options, such as the Mantra. The Mantra will help us raise our vibration which allows us to see everything with the dif-ferent perspective of love being primary (instead of resignation to the closest vibration) which will allow us to make decisions with more *clarity*.

How to the find your Mantra

The answer lies in asking yourself the question without religion, politics, physical attributes, or any thought process with physicality:

Who are you in innocent love, intention, and spiritual *truth*?

One way that **we invite you to find a Mantra** is to understand our examples and our thought processes through them.

Tamara:

I'm Loving Awareness

When I recognize that I'm loving awareness, I remember that I love love. My awareness is loving; that I love my loving awareness, I love how I appreciate, I love who I appreciate, I love appreciating. It's who I am. My ability to appreciate is part of who I am. I love creation, creating, I love the expression of the divine. I love sharing divine experiences with others. It is part of my soul. My whole beingness loves this. How much we love one another in truth is amazing. How much love we are in truth and the love we came with to heal in truth. It's where we're heading: knowing the love that we are and the love that we're going to and remember-ing our truth. In a time and place where it has been missing, it's so beautiful, bountiful, so precious, sacred, needed. The sacredness and memory of our truth is so needed. To build from it, upon it, foundationally is needed. There is so much we can bring into life at this time. We can bring the truth of everything and the love of everything to the forefront because nothing else makes as much sense.

By focusing more on what is true in your life, the truth of who you are, you are finding your Mantra.

ALE:

I CHOOSE LOVE

"I"= Remember the power and energy of the vibration when I say to myself "I"

"Choose" = The possibility of deciding the primary perspective for how I see myself and this world, how I talk to myself, how I talk to others, how I treat myself, others, this world, and everything within it to the best of my ability. I can now define what vibration I want to live in and for how long I can live within it.

"Love" = Harmonizing with the power and energy of the vibration when I say to myself "love", the feeling of it, the smile that comes with the thought of it, a moment in time when I felt it in my totality; an emotional memory that cannot be doubted, of a moment with the divine, of nature, of awe, when I knew that I am a part of everything and everything is part of me, and the feeling layered by more joy because of the ability to repeatedly recognize it with the Mantra.

When you find your Mantra, there is the possibility that you will start repeating it in your mind, start smiling, maybe start saying it out loud, possibly louder and louder, and possibly wanting to dance. This is the beginning of the new experience.

If you already have a spiritual Mantra, the connection of your loving truth correlated with that Mantra can be used in the same aspects.

How to use the Mantra
Steps and Practices

Our Mantras might work for you temporarily or long-term depending on your own experience. Your Mantra might change with the practice of knowing within you what rings the truest about you in love. When you have found your Mantra, these are the steps and practices on how and when to use the Mantra if you find yourself falling into an emotional lull, a feeling that is one that isn't comfortable or totally pleasant.

If you find yourself asking questions or statements while reading the manual or in other moments of life, such as "What is happening?", "Why am I feeling this?", "I'm confused about why my thoughts are going in a direction I don't want", "I'm getting irritated", or, again, with the manual, "Why did I read this the first time and something rang true yet I reread it right after but this time it didn't make sense?", then practice answering your questions with:

"I'm in a negative vibration"
"What is the next step?"

"The next step is to say my Mantra"
"What is my Mantra?"

"_____" (The words that represent your Mantra should be repeated with **intention** in a soft rapid pace whether out loud or within at least four times),

You might then feel yourself getting out of the deeper part of a lull, feeling a *little* lighter. What will happen is a sense of urgency to get out of the lull, thoughts of doubt, confusion, anger, and other negative feelings will come into mind. Why are these thoughts coming in? It is because you are going into higher and higher vibration, though it doesn't seem like it. This isn't because you are doing it wrong, on the contrary, because you are raising your vibration. Each negative vibration that you pass will bring negative thoughts, even some that will make you forget yourself. If you are in, for example, a vibration of despair, by saying the Mantra you might start feeling anger, and then want to stop saying the Mantra because it makes you angry instead of making you feel better, causing you to drop back into despair. This is because with the repetition of the Mantra you went into a different higher than despair vibration (anger) but it is because it is in the process of going to even higher vibrations. By repeating the Mantra you're making your last thought, present thought, and future thought be your loving truth and intention. The other thoughts will come in, but the Mantra will help you go through those thoughts be-cause, in negative energy, the Mantra is also hope. It's a promise that you will be able to get to a better place. It is your LITE.

Focus on harmonized and slow-paced breathing while repeating the Mantra at least four times at a soft rapid pace

but with the memory of what that/those word(s) mean to you. This will allow you to lift yourself out of the lull. Repeat it to yourself until you realize you just felt a profound breath of peace. At this point, when you can, allow yourself to thank the experience, understand it and process the before and after, and rejoice in knowing and acknowledging the truth of yourself and this reality even more. In this moment of higher energy and vibration, repeat the Mantra slowly and remind yourself that this is the vibration in which you want to live.

CHAPTER 1

A THEORY OF HUMANITY

There is light and dark. Infinity and mortality. We are every-thing in one and one in everything. **We are made of energy.** Each Human, each plant, each individual thing on this planet has physical and energetic components of the Universe. We are made out of light of an explosion of energy and the space we see as dark that it fills. If we are made of the same components of the universe, made of energy, in a animal with the brain capacity sufficiently evolved to process this, then we are the Universe recognizing itself within itself.

The theory proposes that the Human is the identical equiva-lent of the Universe within a Mammal Earthling within the Universe itself. This would mean that the Universe, which we are made of physically and energetically in our totality, is recognizing itself in each one of us, each and every gender, with our different genetic make-ups, different bodies, different languages, different cultures, and different insecurities, all within its own self. We are the avatars of this planet for the Universe to experience life within itself with the added capacity to choose our different paths instead of solely instinctual guidance.

The Universe experiences itself through the Human body in energetic emotional waves and recognizes who we are through our harmonization with vibrations through those emotional waves. **The energetic wave movement correlating to emotions and our ability to choose our path because of this wave movement is the divine Human experience.** This theory proposes that Human emotions, thoughts, and physical reactions are correlated to these energetic waves, the emotional vibrations within those waves, the distortions within those vibrations, and the frequency in which we live them.

The intention is to help people navigate their own reality in a different consistent *way*.

Because Humans experience reality through emotions, we must understand what is really happening, asking in the past and present day, "why do we 'feel' this way?", and now also looking at the energetic distortions correlated to vibrations harmonized through wave patterns which explain repeated cycles in our lives.

These wave patterns and vibrations have repeated gears in which we interpret in this reality through emotions, words, memories, problem solving, and more.

The theory proposes the understanding of how they are cyclical symbolic occurrences in this reality and how they can change positively or negatively our own cycle and therefore ours experience on this Earth.

The undulation and dynamic change of the energetic emotional waves, insecurity in all its aspects causing energetic distortions, our sensitivity to the waves of ourselves, others, our past positive and negative experiences being correlated when the vibration is felt, happens to all Humans. It happens because we make it so, consciously, and unconsciously.

The reality we live in and the bodies we live in have instinctual tendencies that causes ourselves to have to understand and process insecurities such as fear, humiliation, rejection, abandonment, loneliness, mortality, sexuality, guilt, anger, shame, and at the same time our instinctual tendencies for love of ourselves and others, joy, liberation, peace, positive and humble self-esteem, sexuality, individuality, value. All this and how it correlates to family, friends, romantic partners, work associates, the environment, our faith, our confidence, basic Human survival, our advancements, and regressions here and everywhere in the world where there are Humans, are challenges all Humans have to confront.

This theory proposes the idea that because Humans are the Universe itself and at the same time physical there is sense of duality in our existence. Infinite and perfect, mortal and imperfect. The Universe created all life and one so evolved that the Universe can recognize itself within itself and can see the beauty and how the Human reacts with high vibrations, appreciating its own perfection. At the same time, the mortal earthling being tired or hungry or thirsty will cause the body to stumble. The Universe, not understanding what it means to stumble, started the process of thinking it did something "wrong" and therefore not only the insecurity of imperfection began, the emotional/energetic Capacitor (commonly called the *ego*) also began to stabilize us and our wave pattern from feeling negative vibrations and at the same time the first distortions started in our harmony even while it helped us create and evolve.

The Universe is eternal and the Human is a mortal Earthling that has an expiration date as almost all life on this planet. We have challenges with death because we know we no longer see the physical aspect of the energy, which causes earthling fear, but at the same time know we are eternal. How can there be this contradiction? It is because we are both, and we know this because we can recognize it. Once we understand this as a possibility, we, as a species, will find a path to end suffering on this earth. That is what it is to be Human: the transition of what we have learned from other species of this earth *survival of the fittest*, to **all should be fit and thriving**.

The Universe has no more need for Human suffering because we have every component we need to make sure we all have the possibility to living our best lives emotionally through vibrational harmony. The Universe suffers when we do yet when we heal the Universe does as well. When we heal ourselves in a vibration we lift others from that same vibration without knowing it, and this is because it is the Universe that sends that energy to the world and, in essence, back to itself. We heal the world by healing ourselves. This theory proposes that we can do this individually and in collective in this reality, in harmony with the environment, our past, our present, our future, ourselves, and others.

CHAPTER 2

WAVE VIBRATIONS AND HUMANS

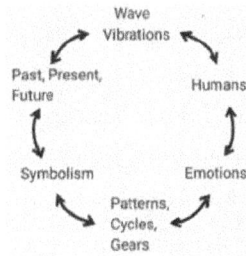

The theory proposes that because we are made of the energy we all live in and are in parallel vibrations with that of the Vibration of Love (VL) and that our distortions or wave movements are translated through emotion. High vibrations and love, low vibrations and insecurity. Multiple and parallel vibrations sometimes happening at the same time. We can and commonly have correlated past negative experiences (insecurity) in a moment that we were in a high vibration (love). This causes wave undulations, like an emotional wave pool going from up to down energetically through vibrations and demonstrating itself emotionally and most likely physically with a form of an Involuntary Discharge of Negative Energy (IDNE). This comes from reaching a certain high vibration that we have correlated with a moment or moments of past insecurity cause or causes distortions in our emotional wellbeing that then also causes a stronger, steeper lull in our wave. The insecurity is an understanding that it wants to be healed to be able to remove the distortion. It is possible and each Human can accomplish this.

Human emotions are the translations of vibrational energies that surround us and are within. When we feel a chang-ing of energy or vibrations or we change vibrations ourselves, the Human thought process of understanding and emotions change. In different environments there are different vibrations: home, school, work, club, etc. that are not only different because they are actual different locations but also because of the energy they reverberate and the Humans in that location with where they are, as well, in their own vibrations. For example: walking voluntarily through an empty temple and walking through into an empty hospital. Some of the thoughts we will have has to do with the ambient energy.

The theory proposes that our emotional stability and wellbe-ing have to do with wave patterns, cycles, and the gears that present themselves at any time, some collective, for example, the first moon landing, yet at the same time unique to each and every Human (the individual perspective of the experience and vibration felt). The reverberation of the emotional vibration of ourselves can possibly be felt by each Human and the environment itself. Because of this vibrational energy and depending on the intentions we have to live our best life, the Universe itself will offer moments or experiences that correlate to our intention and it will happen within a small amount of linear time. It is a way to start lifting our vibrations, self-esteem, and perspective, which advances our lives in timeless ways. It is also possible that in that moment or experience we maintain ourself in negative vibration, which will then maintain itself until the next cycle. It depends on the distortions, the frequency, the insecurities, the understanding we have of ourselves, our focus on the present moment, and the harmony we are in.

The cycles are neither positive nor negative, they depend on us and our perspective on the cycles. There are positive cycles that help us always maintain ourselves in higher vibrations, allowing ourselves to see the gears consciously or unconsciously, take our decisions with balance with our intentions of higher self, our emotional, physical, and spiritual wellbeing in the moment, the possible repercussions (positive/negative with immediate positive results. Being in negative vibrations can cause us to make decisions in insecurity, sometimes necessarily, for the emotional wellbeing in the moment. What is needed might be received, but because it was in negative en-ergy, what might be needed may come with unforeseen distortions. Falling into distortions will not heal the distortions; it only makes them louder. The solution to this is not to blame but adapt, in honesty, to the situation with our true love for ourselves and in positivity being the guide. Our LITE. This will help change our cycle.

The theory proposes the concept of gears within the cycles that will show themselves in a recognizable way and, at the same time, if we are not in the present moment or if we are in the past or future in thought we might see the gear but not recognize it. If recognized at any time the gear will become more evident in its physicality and will pass again through our linear timeline, though we might have to understand the symbolism in our own lives and paths and with balance of our Capacitor ("ego"). When we feel a "click" in our own experience, in positivity, it is the gear changing the cycle to positive. At the same time, a "click" in the contrast can be emotionally destabilizing, but it isn't a direct change to negative. Because of the understanding that the distortions allow us to see it for what it is, which is negative, and with the Mantra, the memory of our own LITE, and **determination in love**, we can voluntarily change the gear to positive. We all can come back to the truth of who we are and advance in that truth in joy.

With understanding of our past, our negative experiences that has caused undulations in our daily life and availability to reach the VL, by being in the in the present in **Determination** in **Love** (not stress to finish), we can see the gears more easily that will allow and help ourselves that much more quickly.

Determination in love (thriving) and *stress-to-finish* (surviving) are two different vibrations with different perspectives and possible outcomes. If we fall into the vibration of *stress-to-finish*, the daily life, the experiences of the moment will have a negative energetic charge of responsibility while the vibration of **Determination in Love** is in harmony with the VL and **can help us have the same stress without the emotional distortions, allowing us to focus with more relaxation, which helps with the quality of the finished project we are Determined in Love to achieve.** There are many reasons we can fall into *stress-to-finish*, such as becoming a parent, economic troubles that could affect dynamics within our life experience, a deadline for a project, etc. There is a possibility with *surviving* to tend to see physicality more, the stress on our faces or of our loved ones, the exhaustion, etc. When we use the mind more than the heart, the Capacitor will activate to support.

When finishing with stress, the energetic vibrational primary reward is relief with the higher self-esteem for our accomplishments being felt later in linear time, while **Determination in Love brings a vibration of higher selfesteem in ourselves instantly and relief secondary but more fulfilling.** They are the wave patterns that we can feel in our daily lives that make life less stressful, more fluid, help us harmonize faster with ourselves and others, our community, the environment, the aspects of our daily life, our joy. **The daily times are when we need the most support. The moment-to-moment things and the small, small things, looking at the positive of the small things, totally is the transformation.** When we transform the small, small everyday things we stress about to positive small things, it is the gear for total transformation and maintenance in the Vibration of Love (VL), turning one symbolic turkey to two. There is no further need to judge ourselves.

The theory proposes that we live in personal vibrations in parallel with the VL. The undulation of our insecurities can have the frequencies of second by second, minute by minute, etc. They go up and down, affected by inner or outside energy, the reaction of us in the moment and where we are vibrationally. There are many more details, for example: how many and what are the insecurities we have at that moment how it affects the Human in that experience that Human is having, if there are others around, if there is sexuality, menstruation, the immediate surroundings, etc., all can affect our ability to get and maintain themselves in harmony with the VL or maintain themselves in a constant higher vibration. Even though there are various vibrations it doesn't mean it is complicated to process. It means that we have to practice how to transform, heal and mute the distortion(s) correlating with the experiences that caused the wave undulations in the first place.

The theory proposes that to do this we must fundamentally understand and integrate these *concepts:*

1. it is possible.
2. understand that now that we know this information, we can now be the voluntary co-creator of their experience on this Earth.
3. we must be sincere with ourselves.
4. we must deactivate the Capacitor for the benefit of ourselves.
5. the time it takes is the time it takes the Universe in that individual Human to understand, and we must respect ourselves and forgive ourselves, always.

To make it easier, the theory proposes to think of insecurities not only as negative emotional vibrations of the lull, but also in levels or grades: superficial (the insecurities that have no emotional affect and can be transformed quickly and positively and is the highest vibration besides having no insecurities whatsoever), light, medium, heavy, total. Each level has to do with the individual Human. What can be "heavy" for some of us might be because of our energetic sensitivity to ourselves and the vibrations around us. If the insecurities are constant and consistent, we might have the Capacitor activated and do not realize it and should be communicated with in a different moment. The closer to total insecurity the more probability of IDNEs we might have.

Total insecurity is a difficult level to get to, and is used as a limit, not an obligation of the contrast. Total insecurity is what we feel during an IDNE, which means it is becoming easier to get to because we are becoming more energetically sensitive, and at the same time, we are remembering our divine selves. We might feel totally in the Vibration/Experience of Love without the obligation of falling into the lull of emotional insecurity, even if we have some (insecurities). The intention is to get to the fluidity of recognizing the falling into a lull so that it becomes so superficial that it has no emotional effect, allowing us to lift ourselves up more easily and quickly and repeatedly at any linear time. To be able to achieve this we must practice processing that when we are feeling the higher vibrations and start to feel undulations three things:

1. **What was the last thought right before the lull?**
2. Use that same thought and expand on it.
3. If the thought isn't available, remember your Mantra.

The theory proposes that in many instances the thought before the lull is what got the Human to the VL and made us vulnerable, and when that happens the insecurity comes in so that we can recognize what needs to be healed to no longer feel that correlating distortion/undulation and stay longer at that vibration. Depending on the grade, it can be easier to more challenging but achievable whatever level. We must remember that the correlation is unique to the Human, to the individual. Even if we feel passion and it correlates to an insecurity of jealousy, depending on the individual, it might be envy or another insecurity formed from the experience of that particular Human, but the theory proposes that in time it will become easier to interpret and therefore easier to *heal*.

In the spiritual energetic perspective:

When we stare at the lull itself
and think about the lull happening, (when we focus on feeling of
the drop into the lull) it is a thought that maintains us in that
vibration,*
aware of higher vibrations *yet*
reaching the higher vibrational thoughts becomes more and more difficult
Drops can possibly feel and be IDNEs.
Support is needed during *this*.
emotional transition of crest to lull (The *Mantra*)

*By recognizing that we are about to fall into the lull our mind has easier access
to remember the higher vibrational thought
before entering it and thinking about the contrast thought.
Practicing thinking; **Practice the Mantra**
taking the higher vibrational thought into the lull makes the lull a softer experience.
its purpose is to heal the vibration.

people have to accept the truth of who they are
their whole complete self

is being grateful to be them, themselves, their true selves,
to be able to express it without *shame*
with its positive and negative aspects in history
shame at being too good at something
shame is the translation of the lull

understanding the dynamics of *love*
the higher vibrations are faster in linear *time*
the lower vibration doesn't want to be felt by the *Human*
higher vibrational thought isn't accessible when focused on the
lower vibrations
easy to allow ourselves to stop reaching
because it takes so much energy
so, the mental process becomes a challenge
that is upsetting and
the confusion is staying in that thought process
and the contrast,
and thinking "this" is the problem.
"this" is the healing of the *contrast*
the thoughts of insecurity/negativity (during lull),
-because they are the last thoughts-
they are newer and easier
for the mind to grab (harmonization in negative energy)
even when they are in the contrast
of the higher vibration
not having access to that thought
that made you so happy
serves the purpose

thinking and taking higher vibrational thought
into the lull (your Mantra)
the lull is *a* softer experience
its purpose is to heal that vibration

The theory proposes the redirection of the lull:

1. someone recognizing that they or others are about to feel a lull
2. if someone does falls into their lull: **tell them only once, with understanding and without arrogance or placation, that they are falling in a lull**
3. if they don't know their Mantra, listen and let them go through it with understanding that they are translating wave patterns of energy/if they do know their Mantra to start repeating it with speed and intention
4. they will process and come back naturally
5. remind them they are understood and remind ourselves or the other about the higher thought that brought them into the lull
6. the knowledge of being listened to by ourselves or by others without being "judged" allows the feeling of value and will lift their vibration solely by knowing they are being heard.

CHAPTER 3

THE EMOTIONAL CAPACITOR (EGO)

The theory proposes that there is an energetic/emotional Capacitor available to the Human that can change vibrations and wave patterns positively about ourselves, other people, animals, the environment, our own surroundings, yet if not harmonized, can also do the same in the contrast. It will be called the "Capacitor" so as to not affect our vibration.

The capacitor is an energetic wave changer that can and activates to absorb negative energy. It's primary function is to evolve, create, and advance, but it has had to be used as well for absorption of negative energy because of the emotional feeling of the energetic lull. The jobs aren't mutually exclusive, one or the other, but because we have had to use the Capacitor to absorb negative energy without understanding the power of our Mantra, it has caused us to live with distortions in some vibrations of our lives. It is commonly called the *ego*, but if we look at the *ego* from this perspective, we can see it is such a powerful negative energy absorber that it has even successfully attained a negative connotation for itself. Its primary objective is our evolution in all aspects of love for ourselves, even when we are in negative vibrations.

When the natural wave movement goes above or below our average vibration the Capacitor will activate, whether be it a thought, a conversation, a mistake, an interesting comment, etc. If we go into a higher vibration, the lull is normally softer, and the Capacitor can be used to permit positive waves and minimize the undulation of the contrast. This is the basis for how we create, evolve, advance. If the wave movement falls into a lull, the Capacitor activates with the possibility of distortions because of activation in insecurity. When we make decisions in this lull of insecurity with the Capacitor activated, they could be beneficial in the short term, but the distortions might cause longer term unexpected repercussions. This could be part of the reason for repeated negative cycles in our lives. (FIG 1, page 45)

THE OVERACTIVE CAPACITOR

The Capacitor can also be used to permit negative energy and minimize the undulation of the *supposed* contrast, even against our own well-being. This can happen when our Capacitor starts to become overactive. It is overly trying to maintain ourselves in higher vibrations while dealing with energetic distortions from having to activate because of negative energy. This can also happen in higher vibration, when the physical becomes secondary to the higher vibration, also possibly being against the long term emotional and physical wellbeing of us. When the Mantra can be practiced and understood in harmony, we can allow the Capacitor to allow ourselves the ability to listen to the positive with positive emotion and listen to the negative with understanding and filtration of pertinent information with easier ability to maintain/react in higher vibrations. With the Capacitor overactive it can cause us to from having previously guided the Capacitor with balance that was maintained with self-understanding, accepting advice from others in all aspects, and in a high vibration, to reach the point that we follow directly the guide of the Capacitor itself while it is in a moment of over-absorbing negative energy and distortions, and follow it though it is in a place without discretion, hesitation, strategy, or thorough thought process for our well-being, whether be it emotional or physical.

In turn this action starts the reaction of change in the wave dynamic, causing us to believe in only our decisions, possibly impulsively and with conviction, without balance of full conceptual understanding of our actions, reactions, and repercussions. The vibration that we live in might start changing and a negative cycle might start to repeat itself. We might lose the ability of understanding and gain the desire of resistance or rebellion, our Capacitor stuck in its position to allow only reflections of positive vibrations of our desire and our goal, possibly even against our own wellbeing or morality. Those of us going through this process might sometimes be prevented from un-derstanding during this time. When we realize an imperfection has been made, and there is the possibility of feeling out of balance, the overactive Capacitor will absorb both positive and negative waves from outside our own mind, and at the same time reflect positive waves from inside our own mind and only accept positive waves from others if it is limited to the vibrations we want, even if we have added distortions within those vibrations.

The theory proposes that this might cause us to maintain our belief structure and rhythm, decision-making through either erroneous information or impulsiveness or rebellion, causing us to be blind and deaf to the outside world, and possibly blind and deaf to our own well-being. This changes the dynamic from being the energetic/emotional Capacitor that is avail-able to help us to a cycle of us defending the Capacitor against others and then against ourselves, causing disruption, distor-tions, and possibly the regression and/or repetition of a cycle instead of a cycle of evolution.

Why this possibly happens is because if we allow ourselves to overpower our ability to admit imperfections we might possibly make more, causing an aggregate of vibrational distortions. To then admit to them could cause a sensation of not only feeling the fall into a lower vibration but the possibility of not being able to get out of it, the fear of collapse, a lull that feel like that of a tsunami of negative energy, distortions, multiple changes of negative vibrations, and fear in our own minds, and that might be more than we would want to accept. It is logical that we might maintain our course in contrast to our benefit, but the fear comes from both the mortal earthling aspect and from the emotional vulnerability from past experiences with guilt (whether we put it on ourselves or it was imposed by others from a young age) when the vibration and distortions were first recorded. The vibrational change of admission of imperfection to ourselves or to others has been taken advantage of by others, because of the vibration correlation throughout the chain of history. A possible catalyst is negative reinforcement and/or manipulation during these moments of vulnerability. This theory proposes that the emotional Capacitor must be harmonized from the earliest age possible so that admission of imperfection from learning on this earth isn't used to cause insecurities, as Humans have used them before (chapter Guilt), and that in itself will allow us all to evolve even faster.

The theory proposes that the Capacitor can get to this level because our history of the contrast has been overpowering. Humans, through negative vibrations in all their aspects, have felt so much shame and guilt when they realize they are out of harmony with the Capacitor to defend ourselves and the primary reaction might be reflection: manipulating others and their paths because we know they other cannot defend themselves, and instead of helping one another we have taken advantage, adding distortions to ourselves. Another reason that we haven't been able to admit that they can't harmonize their own Capacitor and that we are out of balance is because throughout history we have given more negative reinforcement for imperfection than positive reinforcement of self-awareness. The method that was used on us, if we follow the same cycle, will most likely be the method we used on others. It isn't conscious; it is lack of our own awareness. When we reflect our overactive Capacitor on each other if there is one, our Capacitor will reverberate energy back to us quicker to support. Unconsciously and sometimes consciously we can realize this, and we as Humans, in that moment, we have chosen to help, have chosen to hinder, or have chosen to ignore ourselves.

The theory proposes that awareness, self-awareness, and positive reinforcement are primary. Positive reinforcement isn't always saying *yes*, it is guidance to appreciate the advancement of learning and creation and teaching ourselves to learn and create positive ways on how to adapt to negative experiences. Responsibility for our words and actions is a positive. It allows us to experience, learn, appreciate, accept guidance in positive vibrations. Responsibility for our responsive actions, when in a high vibration, is also a positive, because it allows us to fundamentally appreciate the appreciation in the highest vibration.

We can energetically change the vibration so that we can emotionally remove the insecurity (the undulation of our wave) from our past negative experiences. The concept of "forgive and forget" is to forgive everything that has to do with that insecurity, from our actions, even innocent, in that experience. The concept of forgetting is transforming/muting the distortion that has been correlated to that experience, not forgetting that experience itself: transformation that starts the cycle of healing. The more we remember the transformed version over time the experience might be totally distant even though it caused emotional distress in the moment. The ability to recognize the moment with no vibrational emotional connection will allow us to maintain ourselves in higher vibrations for longer periods of linear time. The intention is to understand that our healing is the reason. The forgiving of our past pain can become the healing of our future joy.

With forgivingness of the overactive Capacitor, forgiveness of not being able to see clearly, understanding, and outlining future actions emotionally we can remind ourselves of this very moment what we want to achieve: balance and life experience in the highest vibration possible.

Limiting our negative energy intake is positive, though we must define what is considered negative or positive to the individual. When we suggest unasked advice to another, the Human might take this negatively or with the insecurity of judgement of ourselves or the other or both. If we look at this aspect of the theory, what that person is doing is explaining how another Human was able to get to a higher vibration for them, though it might be lower vibration for the explained. This causes disruption, a lull, and the Capacitor to activate itself.

The theory proposes that when we record a moment of insecurity when we are open to love, the insecurity that is recorded plays its note in our harmony and it causes distortion, and we can possibly take it personally, or blame another, reflecting because of the mind body vibration correlation. When the awareness and recognition of finding those distortions in our vibrations are maintaining their correlation repeatedly, it is a reflection of ours that is being sent and therefore an insecurity that can be healed by understanding, forgiveness, dropping that particular note and not the song, and harmonizing with ourselves again. Transformation.

The theory proposes that if we make a mistake, we can ask ourselves to first take emotion out of the equation and focus on facts: the action(s), reaction(s), repercussion(s). There is no blame, there is no judgement, but there is always the possibility of taking responsibility for our own actions for our own emotional benefit, not for anyone else's by force. It also doesn't mean to allow ourselves to be open in total vulnerability and total deactivation of the Capacitor, because in this moment negative reinforcement within ourselves or through others has been a catalyst for some of our emotional pain/energetic distortions. Just the acceptance of the action(s), reaction(s), and repercussion(s) will allow us to advance into understanding and adapting in positivity.

With the understanding that, for example, we are excited to start a project and are in a higher vibration, we might fall into a lull of confusion or insecurity. There is also the possibility of physicality temporarily becoming clumsier. If the Capacitor is also activated, it also allows us to harmonize with the crest of the VL and when there is a lull, no matter how slight, the thought of falling from the vibration might overwhelm the ability to hear and/or process instructions. There is the possibility of a feeling of impatience for feeling that a lull is about to take place. In this case, we should ask ourselves to harmonize in patience for the long-term benefit of achieving the goal of longer-term harmonizing with the VL.

With this in mind, we will be able to go back to the higher vibration with understanding, love, and Determination in Love, and it is a cycle that will progress in being able to maintain ourselves in that vibration with the Capacitor processing in a different way, opening up possibilities of better self-understanding and awareness.

How does this correlate to the *Mantra?*

The Mantra is a way to help balance the Capacitor in our life experience. It will allow the Capacitor to evolve and create with more ease. Because the Mantra can support the Capacitor in lifting us into higher vibration, the Capacitor can function with more clarity by relieving it of one of its main jobs of supporting us through all negative energy, allowing it to focus on our joy and ability to live our best life. The ability to remind us of our loving truth of ourselves has always been here though we hadn't realized how powerful it can be in our life experi-ence. With practice the Mantra and the Capacitor will start to work in harmony and not only will the lulls be softer and easier to process but our Capacitor will be liberated to focus solely on our spiritual evolution in love, supported by our LITE. This is when creativity in all types of art can happen. Sometimes it is taking the love vibration into a project and focusing the love into the project to allow us to heal in a way that brings focus on something physical to help heal the emotional. Our LITE in physicality created by us and for us to remember and appreciate who we are and it comes from U.

FIGURE 1

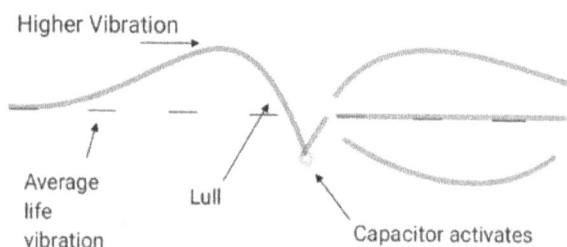

Higher Vibration

Average life vibration

Lull

Capacitor activates

FIGURE 2

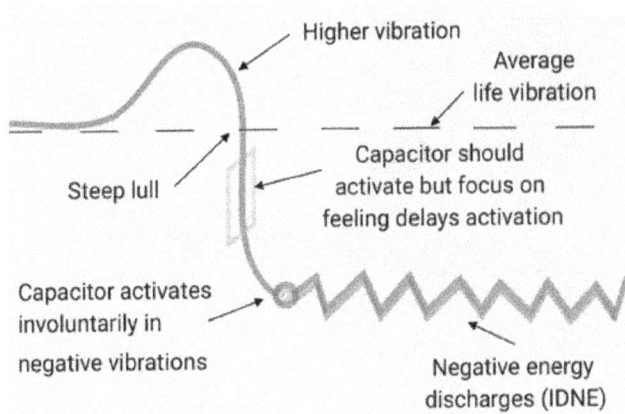

Higher vibration

Average life vibration

Capacitor should activate but focus on feeling delays activation

Steep lull

Capacitor activates involuntarily in negative vibrations

Negative energy discharges (IDNE)

CHAPTER 4

INVOLUNTARY DISCHARGES OF NEGATIVE ENERGY (IDNEs). *A.K.A PANIC/ANXIETY ATTACKS*

The theory proposes the change of the term *panic/anxiety attack* to **Involuntary Discharge of Negative Energy** (IDNE) due to the understanding of energy and the correlation to the Human. Our normal wave pattern, if we go into a higher vibration, will go into a lower vibration naturally. When this happens, our Capacitor will activate to bring us back up into higher vibration (FIG 1, page 44). If we go into higher vibration and then the lull of going into the lower vibration is steep, we can feel it more intensely. If we focus on the feeling of the lull, our Capacitor activates later, and we harmonize involuntarily in a lower vibration causing us added distortions.

This involuntary harmonization to a negative vibration causes an Involuntary Discharge of Negative Energy (IDNE), or the beginning of what was considered a panic or anxiety attack (FIG 2, page 23). When this happens, and because we are mammal earthlings, we go into survival mode, *flight*, or *fight*. Because of these instincts, when we have a IDNE we want to physically leave the situation, room, location, city, etc., because of *flight*, and because it is in our own minds, we don't know how to *fight* so we start to react in different ways: primal fear, primal thoughts of violence and physicality, mistrust in ourselves and others, paranoia, total loss of harmony. This is a Mortal Earthling reaction to the loss of *control* of ourselves. This discharge of energy that is in a negative vibration correlate to a state of emergency for the Human if we don't realize what it is.

When we can recognize this reaction is occurring, there are steps and practices that will help us lift ourselves into higher vibration. After we harmonize with our LITE, we can start to understand what was happening, why it was happening, what was the insecurity, and the location it happened, how we felt beforehand, any physical memories (tingling of the nose, etc.) that will advise ourselves. We can start conceptualizing in a different way that will allow us as Humans to process this energy without negative emotional distortions or connections. When we can make this a positive habit (the intention of understanding, learning, appreciating the moment, small positive things instead of admonishment for falling the vibration) we are allowing others to know they can feel the joy of the higher vibration who are feeling the contrast in this moment. If the other feels trust within the moment, it will allow all us to feel thankfulness right after and in the future, witnessing the transformation to love and the experience and joy of it.

When we start having an IDNE, whether ourselves or another, by simply recognizing it possibly happening, the possibilities flow in the positive. *The Mantra Reference Page* and these next steps should be considered a reference for a way to make an IDNE voluntary.

If processing this before an IDNE happens, we send an invitation to be in a place where we feel emotionally safe, physically comfortable, by ourselves or if others are around, that they be those who are trusted. With these small details covered we can begin to integrate this process more easily. If processing this while an IDNE is happening, the steps are the same.

Ask and answer to the best of your ability these 6 questions:

1. Where are you?
2. Do you consider it a safe place?
3. Who are you with?
4. If you are with others, do you trust them?
5. What are you doing?
6. Is it acceptable or more than acceptable?

Here are three examples:

I am at home by myself reading a book

I am at a social gathering singing with my friends

I am at the store with a friend buying things

First example:

Where are you? I am at home.

Do you consider it a safe place? Yes

Who are you with: I am by myself

If you are with others, do you trust who are with? n/a

What are you doing? I'm reading a book.

Is it acceptable or more than acceptable? Yes, I like to read.

You are in a safe place by yourself doing something that you like. You are having an IDNE because you feel that nothing can harm you in this moment and are releasing energy for your emotional benefit later in life. This feeling wasn't intentional, it just wasn't understood why it was happening. By understanding this you will start to increase your energy. By adding your repetition of the Mantra at this time you will be able to get out of the IDNE faster and live happier for longer periods of linear time. Integrating the knowing that you are allowing yourself to emotionally process a change in your wave dynamic for your best benefit is inspiration for all Humanity.

Second example:

Where are you? I am at a social gathering.

Do you consider it a safe place? I can't answer that now; next question

Who are you with? My friends

If you are with others, do you trust who you are with? Yes, they are my friends

You are at a social gathering with people you trust. Can you now consider the location safe? Yes

What are you doing? I'm about to sing.

Is it acceptable or more than acceptable? I love singing!

You are in a safe place with people you trust doing something you love. You are having an IDNE because you feel that nothing can harm you in this moment and this moment was meant for you to celebrate and release energy in positivity. You deserve this moment of joy. By understanding this you will start to increase your energy. By adding repetition of the Mantra at this time you will be able to get out of the IDNE faster and live happier for longer periods of linear time. Know that you are allowing yourself to emotionally process a change in your wave dynamic for your best benefit is inspiration for all Humanity.

Third example:

Where are you? I'm at the store.

Do you consider this a safe place? I don't know; I don't think so.

Who are you with? I am with my friend.

If you are with others, do you trust those you are with? Yes.

You are in a store with a friend that you trust.

Can you consider yourself in a safe place with your friend? My friend is supporting me.

What are you doing? Buying things.

Is that acceptable or more that acceptable? Yes.

You are in a supermarket with a friend you trust doing something acceptable. You are having an IDNE because there is a part of you that feels that you are in a safe place that can discharge energy though you don't consciously understand why. The focus now should be understanding that you are in a lull, and at this time repeat your Mantra to get out of the IDNE faster and give you the opportunity to process from a different vibration and perspective. Just the acknowledgement of what you are feeling and being able to process the steps is remarkable in itself and helps us all evolve.

Other possibilities of why the IDNE happened in this example include the Capacitor cannot handle any more negative energy and needs to release in the moment that some safety and comfort is possible, the supermarket being a public place feels unconsciously safer than a private setting, or the vibration the person was experiencing correlated to one that had a distortion that needed to be healed, etc.

Emotional Instability is Energetic Sensitivity.

We are feeling our energetic waves. We are recognizing our divinity in physicality.

The theory proposes practice on maintaining positive energy in the lull. The Mantra is allowing ourselves to appreciate ourselves without fear or resistance. To be alive and doing that is monumental moment in our life experience, and can dramatically change how we, as Humans, handle things emotionally. The theory proposes that not all IDEs are negative. If we are harmonized, in positive energy, an IDE might happen and instead of a flight or fight it would be celebrate and rejoice, the idea of dancing in the moment comes to us (even without music), o smile to ourselves, or skip instead of a walk, or stopping and praying, etc. It is a positive IDE that appreciates what we are feeling emotionally and energetically and is transformed easily and possibly with excitement to voluntary. This also supports those who are in the contrast. When we laugh and clap or hit our knee, it is us reminding us that not only can we be in a higher vibration and in physicality at the same time temporarily, we can live in it.

"Where am I?"

"Who am I with?"

"What am I doing?"

"I am having a IDNE"

"Mantra", "Mantra", "Mantra" "Mantra" (for as long as it takes)

"Thank you, thank you, thank you"
"When I'm ready I will question why, forgive it, and live life happier in true joy"

This is possible and achievable through patience and practice. You will harmonize faster and faster in linear time until you always have beautiful DE in high vibrations, a rewarding repeatable opportunity for the Human.

In all the examples, though not stated when getting out of the IDNE in the moment, there is a correlation: there is a distortion that needs to be healed in order to maintain yourself in higher vibrations for longer periods of time. These aren't judgements or punishments, they are energetic distortions that can be healed by forgiving, transforming, muting, and maintaining them in the vibrations they are in, so you no longer hear them in your harmony. These steps and the Mantra Reference page form a possibility of making an IDNE voluntary so that we can eventually harmonize with ourselves as quickly as possible.

Asking yourself the questions,

"What was the last thought before the insecurity?"
"What was the insecurity?"

can help demonstrate a wave crest and wave lull, respectively; one to surf and the other to transform for the next wave, or in another perspective, mute the note in our harmonies and remove the distortion. Transformation is the evolution of love.

When you are ready to start harmonizing and muting distortions, the theory proposes this as a reference as well:

1. remind ourselves of where we started, our community, the people around us, the ideologies, the idea of ourselves, the environment, the vibrations, and question the struggle, the challenge, the part that is trying to be pushed past.

2. remind ourselves who were we destined to be when we were born/crowned, what do we want in love in our life experience

3. allow the mourning and muting of the emotional distortions of the challenge by being in Determination in Love and embracing our Humanity, as individuals and as one

4. understanding the yearning of consistency with a limitless shapeshifting future of possibilities, all with firm emotional foundations, like a prism: choices with a strong supported system.

5. The harmonization and center of ourselves is the temple that holds us together, the liberal expression of us, in our temple and out of it, brings an awareness back to where we started, our community, the people around us, our ideologies, the idea of ourselves, the environment, the vibrations, and the answer of why the struggle, why the challenge, the part that is trying to be pushed past is no longer forced because we have become our expanded self, it has been recognized, it has been understood, and it has been forgiven, as we have with ourselves.

If we look at this in the spiritual energetic perspective:
overcoming the "stuckness" of old programming
for your new destiny of being mourning to let go
being open to new possibilities in one's own temple
within ourselves
have the experience of intention/belief
part of the divine had to split to the contrast
the angel and the contrast to know itself
to understand that they come and manifest as sounds
but they are vibrations as the contrast
because of an awareness of itself
that its purpose was divine love
that's the reason for that existence.
it makes it complete.
and the lull could just be "the lull" as the reason.
we can't know one without the other,
the negativities from the lull,
the transformation for it, for Humanity,
that understanding of it all.
in some sense of the term the VL
the expanded experience can be an emotional memory.
even if lived once it can be gift
not having to have it anymore
only in a moment in time
but it isn't part of our experience
it's the healing of that experience
that now has to be understood right now as what has to happen
because divine awareness expanded

didn't know sadness
recognizes it as itself
it does everything it can to preserve so that it can come back to
appreciate its conception
it had to understand compassion
not judging the emotional Humans that we are, the things we
have done in the contrast,
to take the most beautiful parts and use them to create with,
but when we realize the emotional contrast
we can leave that and celebrate having healed it.
anger might come out, but it is part of our history.
We wouldn't really understand
we will go through the stages of mourning
mourning process of us being authentic,
but see it in its beauty and to see it in the VL that everything
comes from,
even the negative vibrations come from that same love,
and that's who we are,
it's all in our DNA

the mind was seen as the *bad* guy,
it was protecting our heart,
the forgiveness of the words and
not taking things personally and
taking in sounds and lights and past experiences
in memory and in DNA.
in terms of just doing living this life
with just a heart
there was no thinking

it was just repressed wanting (from not understanding ourselves as the Universe in the Human, the Human/Mortal
Earthling sexuality, mortality, power over ourselves and others, joy, communion, admitting imperfection and still be considered perfect to ourselves and others in our learning and
appreciation, and so much more)
this and the vibration of love
their effects in correlations
and apart,
the mind
coming in connection with the heart,
allowed a way to discern a bit more
move in a slower, lighter way,
to appreciate the experiences.
but it's now time to embrace the beauty
of the truth of it and let go of the rest.
we associated karma with negative
transform to
our mind is our good karma
we are our co-creators
heart holds emotions (vibrations and distortions)
mind holds transformed past (harmony and creation)
that's karma living it's experience
why have we been doing to ourselves. The contrast...
recognize the contrast,
the purpose of earth is connect in truth
coming full circle...
transition transformation integration

CHAPTER 5

GUILT AND ITS NEGATIVE EFFECTS, PRACTICES/
HABITS (POSITIVE AND NEGATIVE), TRUE
FORGIVENESS

The theory proposes that guilt is a powerful vibration unto
itself, and it can also be a distortion. It is one of the easiest
vibrations to harmonize with in a lull and correlate with the
VL if we believe we caused ourselves or another Human suffering without intent, made decisions in the lull that had repercussions with distortions, or we feel we don't deserve the
higher vibration we are feeling, but **forgiveness is stronger in
every aspect**. Guilt can also possibly be the repercussion of being harmonized with the VL and being obligated by ourselves
(because of habit or old programming) or another to feel that
we shouldn't feel the vibration we are in. It is in contrast of
our own intentions of love, or for believing that we shouldn't
be in the VL for so long, or that we don't deserve long term
happiness, even though all these thought processes are in con-

trast. The distortion of guilt has been used as a method to lower our or another's vibration, an unconscious lull that we put ourselves in to possibly placate another or placate ourselves. It is a note that we can put in our harmony and correlate to our lull quite easily. It can cause challenges in decision making without distortions from the insecurity of the guilt itself. **Guilt has been used to manipulate ourselves and by others** for their own motives. Humans have used religions, the society, the family, etc. because of the potential of allowing us to be vulnerable constantly, constantly having to recognize our imperfections, possibly getting to the point of resigning our actions and decisions to others, with total lack of process of any repercussions to our actions, allowing our Capacitor to deactivate in the contrast, absorbing any distortions whatsoever, or resign ourselves to harmonize with a vibration/perpetual feeling of guilt. The insecurities come when we think they might have hurt themselves or others, and because of the intention of maintenance in higher vibrations, the Capacitor will activate until it can recognize the possibility (even if fictitious).

The theory proposes that guilt can come from two sides: the distortions of *blame* (ourselves or others), and acceptance of the distortions of *blame* in our harmony (from ourselves or others). We have been programmed that **change**, even for the wellbeing of ourselves, is a challenge, even if for the positive. Solely for being a **change** in our routine, it can cause insecurity in the moment of decision when presented with an experience to do so (cycles and gears). There is a possibility that we can take this in a negative and cause us to want to change the vibration with an impulse which in turn can change it and it also changes the focus of what was wanted to be changed in the first place. This can cause us to feel guilt for not being able to complete the task, recording distortions with intentions, making us feel that it is useless to make an effort when we will finish feeling negative vibrations, which is what is happening, but because of the distortion vibration correlation, not the self-motivation or emotional strength within ourselves.

The theory proposes self-understanding, linear time, and space until we can make the intention again in **Determination in Love**. If the correlating distortions aren't at least recognized (they don't have to be completely healed to make positive decisions that correlate with the intentions) it can possibly perpetuate a negative cycle. Accepting responsibility voluntarily for our words, actions, and energies makes guilt be a vibration and distortion that we no longer have to feel and an energy that can no longer be used to manipulate our lulls. We can know the truth of any negative repercussions. This can be healed by harmonizing with our Capacitor in understanding of intentions and the practice of using your Mantra when in the vibration or feel the energy of guilt.

In the spiritual energetic perspective:

awareness of feeling the "need to control" our emotions

challenge to "control" our emotions
passionate or sensitive
one tries to "control" it
love being, reacting positive or negative was seen as *bad*
"learn to control your emotions"
sometimes we didn't have "control" of our emotions
everything that happens is love or a call to love
the parts we play are amazing
we should appreciate that
not being able to control
and then not understand why
we're trying to understand
we were *judging* instead of taking time to understand
judging puts things in an energy that doesn't get resolved
questions that needs to be answered
a solution to the challenge
blaming or judging dismisses the possibility of solution
love puts spotlight on the challenge and sees it as something
that needs to be resolved
take it as beautiful
what is needed to support this
let go of "control" and start to "harmonize"
action that should be automatic but is not
the Capacitor absorbing negative energy
is an adaption to an experience that is no longer needed
Transformation
Constantly evolving to the highest vibrational self.
Not the highest vibration as the purpose.

It is the most satisfying experience of self and self is love
Love is Self-wanting to connect with others and
having a completely different experience in our moment-to-moment life.
in terms with the individual and
how we react with the collective
the possibilities are endless
the thing that was missing was the dynamics that also came from Humanity
Angels and Humans together.
this expansion was including all of us and Humanity healing itself
Circle catching up with itself

The theory proposes that practices and habits can be positive and negative, depending on how it allows us to advance ourselves. If the habits have any type of distortion, guilt, etc., that is from within, we must find a way to adapt the habit to positivity. Transformation. The cycle of the positive habit can allow us to live in higher vibrations for longer periods of linear time and become practices.

The vocabulary we use might be one of the most important aspects of a Human's life.

Each word that we speak as Humans not only has a significance for each person but at the same time has an energy/vibration within it that can impact others in a way we might not have been able to process (until now). For example, the word "abuse", said out loud or inward, can cause an immediate lowering of our vibration and/or cause distortions within ourselves, a possible IDNE, etc., solely by what that word means to each individual Human and the energy behind it.

Because of this understanding the vocabulary we use with ourselves and out loud might have reactions we didn't expect of ourselves or others or others not expecting their own reaction. It might cause repercussions that might cause distortion(s) for all involved in that moment. When we use a word like, "crazy" or "unbelievable" or "incredible", we are telling ourselves unconsciously "I am crazy if I accept this in my reality", "this is not believable in my reality", "this is not credible in my reality", etc., negating what we have been witness to in our experience in life.

It is the lull, the insecurity of believing something that we know we witnessed but the doubt that nobody would believe us and so how can we believe, unconsciously judging ourselves in a wave lull that happens right after being in the VL by ourselves or with others, possibly with the Capacitor activated in that moment and because of feeling the VL the Capacitor might use the contrast to try to balance.

Feeling the VL to immediately telling ourselves it's "unbelievable" to maintain the vibration we are in which (to equilibrate contrasts) is solely a transformation of practice and vocabulary, allowing the experience and us enjoying it harmonization with understanding that our reality has so much more to offer.

The theory proposes that the Capacitor might be protecting us from negative distortions in the lull, it isn't conscious, it is to protect from disillusionment and the possible feeling of *judgement* of imperfection in trusting in the VL A change in vocabulary to "Amazing" "Wonderful" "Awe-inspiring" "Beautiful", etc. will allow us to process the experience without negation of the experience for ourselves and for others.

One of the most important practices we can have is to be aware of how we talk to ourselves, and from there, to others. If we talk negatively to ourselves, not only is it difficult to face challenges and achieve objectives in Determination in Love, but if another starts to speak negatively to us, it means two people are sending negative vibrations and distortions, one being ourselves. The reverberation of that vibration also is sent out, possibly being received by others who are in that vibration, and at that moment we might become vulnerable to the manipulation of others. When completing our objective, in *stress to finish*, we will only look at the mistakes, the doubts, the negative experiences that passed, the high self-esteem or proudness of ourselves becomes more difficult to feel, out of habit of how we talk to ourselves, which can lead to the possibility of communicat-ing with others in the same way we talk to ourselves. This can cause us to feel guilty and the Capacitor to activate to protect ourselves if the negativity comes from within and outside, which can cause a habit to maintain itself in a negative cycle.

The theory proposes to always talk to ourselves with love and intentions of love and not negative reinforcement, cordiality and politeness, respect for ourselves and others, patience, forgiveness, and the understanding that it is a process and it takes the time it takes for each of us.

We dance in vibrations to harmonize... when we are obligating ourselves or another to change the vibration instead of harmonizing with the vibration wanted, this is judgement/manipulation. If we talk down to ourselves, we are trying to change our vibration consciously and unconsciously. Whether this is done through the habit of putting us in a vibration that we are comfortable in because of past experiences in our lives depends on the Human. If we must talk down to ourselves or treat ourselves with lack of respect and judgement, we are creating our own reverberation of negative energy and believing we are solely victim of it when we are both the victim and the present moment perpetrator.

The theory proposes that we, as Humans, have not understood this reasoning before, and the guilt of us doing this to ourselves without understanding the inner dialogue we have built through our experiences of our lifetime can cause IDNEs, wave distortions, and/or the Capacitor to activate or over activate (possibly in a negative tone because of the vibration, thereupon showing itself as its own example of us being in that vibration). It is a reflection of insecurity that can be healed by accepting the possibility, forgiveness for not understanding before because no one has, and removing the emotional vibrational distortion from the past experience itself. It is not necessary to forget the experience if we do not want to for its learning experience, and if this option is taken, it is recommended to use the references in the chapter IDNE and feel confident that the emotional vibrational distortion of the experience is no longer there unless through empathy of others telling of their experiences. In this aspect, the Capacitor can allow us to be empathetic or sympathetic to the experience and the feeling, understanding the suffering without harmonizing with the vibration itself and its correlating emotional effects.

The theory proposes that when we begin to talk to ourselves with love of who we are as a Human, it transforms a negative habit into positive practice. When we change our vocabulary or remember or realize when we are talking to ourselves in a negative way, understand that it is a process and forgive ourselves, and when we start being profoundly proud of ourselves, each transformation lifts the vibrations of ourselves and every other Human in that vibration. In time it will cause more tension and energy to talk negatively to ourselves and others, demonstrating in a beautiful way the respect we remembered to have for ourselves, transforming the world, our joy in the moment, our future, and the future of others, simply with a word and intention.

The theory proposes that profound forgiveness, vibrational forgiveness, with the intentions of allowing **ourselves and/ or other Humans** be able to remove a correlational distortion of vibrational and emotional insecurity with the love we have with ourselves and/or the other Humans, without intentions of manipulation in any form neither in the present nor the future, is one of the most powerful decisions we, as Humans, can choose to do. The power of insecurity is strong, but forgiveness is stronger. We can harmonize with the feeling of availability to be vulnerable and at the same time feel accepted for our imperfections with the understanding of our learning of ourselves and/or the feelings of others, without judgement. We can feel the Vibration/Experience of Love completely, muting distortions or even harmonizing totally through the understanding that we are in an imperfect world and that we're loved for our perfection of being the Universe in learning. The balance of our Capacitor will in turn renew itself in a more intense form that supports the positive advancement of the life and experience of ourselves and/or others because of the healing.

The theory proposes that forgiveness in that way can transform, give permission, open a different perspective, and harmonize in the energy of the purpose of our lives. In other words, the reaction is the reason for the transformation of ourselves and at the same time others. The theory invites the concept of letting us have the new experience of healing a pain or distortion of the past in the same vibration. While we can recognize the purpose of the contrast (the insecurity), instantly the format that we have the experience and life with other changes, changing the contrast (the insecurity) to its contrast (the Vibration/Experience of Love). There is the possibility of a mourning for recognition of the past, and that must be forgiven as well to advance in the positive for ourselves and all Humans in that vibration.

The theory proposes that what we didn't understand until now is that it was a well of appreciation of the purpose that it served. There are levels of appreciation that we still haven't processed yet as Humans, but they allow us to be free and be able to create without resistance nor distortions. We couldn't appreciate the process until we understood the process.

In the spiritual energetic perspective:

decisions in the confusion of the lull have caused a lot of damage understanding its purpose
love can naturally evolve from the contrast
the awareness of the lull and the transformation
the more painful experience in the contrast
is the most joyous experience in the VL when transformed
what is the emotional equivalent of that vibrational distortion if placed in the positive?
what is the perfect emotional contrast?
transform the experience of it.

expanded version of what created the lull goes back and forth
and becomes more beautiful and dynamic
this is how it works
allows everyone to become their truth; to become their self,
even those who have had a difficult time, of being scared.

The theory proposes that profound appreciation or thank-fulness, like forgiveness, is a powerfully energetic vibration that can change our lives and others in negative vibrations. Profound appreciation given from us to us and/or to others sends a vibration that, because of negative past experiences, guilt, lack of self-worth, imposed humility, is so strong it makes it a challenge to accept without distortions. We can feel that we don't deserve the energy of that vibration because we are imperfect (as we all are and at the same time perfect), we think of reasons for not accepting the appreciation, etc. **It is solely a lull of insecurity after a beautiful harmonization with the VL**, though because it is a lull it might activate the Capacitor when it isn't necessary but impedes a vibration sent with love in a different energy and form. When we accept appreciation totally, the energy of both sides (the appreciator and the appreciated even if us to ourselves) lifts the vibration for all involved in the experience and for other Humans. When we give profound appreciation, we will feel vulnerable but at the same time we will feel the power of the energy of the vibration of thankfulness. It is the intention of us to live that way, in every moment, vulnerable and strong in the Vibration of Love knowing that we have the energy to receive and give without insecurities allowing us to live our lives in higher vibrations. When we pray, meditate, stare at the sunset, look at the stars, when we connect this way with ourselves and others, we can feel the energy and understand what it means to be living in vibrations.

In the spiritual energetic perspective:

staying in that secure environment
insecurity came with the vibrations (lulls to *IDNEs*)
interpretations don't have access
to the higher vibrational experiences
the communication of the lower and higher vibrations
understand the expansiveness of love
we thought we couldn't live it otherwise
the understanding that the vibration
is in the reason why we make those decisions
so by living in those vibrations
we had to learn compassion from first and second-hand experience.
empathy and compassion which is a different experience
or love that was known in us coming together
physical and spiritual
it was confusing
but first understood,
the ability to learn compassion,
then started feeling, understand why people
have those feelings and thoughts

it all makes sense
because it allows us to interact
in the most beautifully possible way
but we had to learn the dynamics
of each other from this perspective,
which is really ourselves
coming back together with ourselves
on many levels of interpretation.
as we get closer
it becomes more and more healed,
we know that they are the most satisfying experiences
understanding what we are learning
in the richness, depth of quality
of the experience, and the coming together is what is the most
important.
in the Universe it was expansion,
then contraction,
we were, until now, living in the contrast,
it is our turn,
as Humans, as the Universe,
to expand in quality and richness
depthness of experience in love
with the awareness
of the perfection of it all.
It is a personal willingness,
as we get to this place,
moment to moment start to become all there is,
until we are all in that place together,

the interactions between each other,
how it gets set up,
now we are going to go back to the contrast
with an awareness of it all,
that is going to lead
to a new experience of our lives.
constant expansion in love
the speed will be transformed reinterpreted
we get to be aware
in our part of this creation.
gratitude and appreciation of love is so high

CHAPTER 6

THE IMPULSE, "CONTROL", FORGIVE FORGET
& QUESTION

The theory proposes that the easiest example to understand how we live in waves is the emotional movement of the impulse. The action of following the impulse, whether be it from another person or ourselves, lifts us quickly into a different vibration because of the spontaneity, though it could be the contrast, and lowers us quickly into a different vibration because of the spontaneity. What then happens is the reaction in a wave lull, possibly being the contrast (from a total "yes" to a thought of an absolute "no", possibly coming into the mind just as quickly as the initial impulse). **It is important for us to remember the thought that came in after the lull and to recognize it isn't a total negation of the impulse; it is ourselves assuring our vibrational wellbeing in the present moment and after.** Because of the instantaneous of it, the well-being should be thought about to the point of self-introspection. The theory proposes that the quick fall into the lull can affect us because of past experiences, the distortions of guilt, and also where we are vibrationally in the moment, etc. The Universe wants us to enjoy life, at the same time take care of us not only with the impulse but also with the reactions and repercussions that follow (positive, negative, or neutral). Depending on how vulnerable we are to other Humans, whether be it through words, vibrations, etc., the impulse could be fun in the moment but the repercussions, without thought process, could be negative, causing us to record a distortion of not being able to enjoy impulses without negative feelings afterward, or feelings of guilt put on ourselves or imposed by others. There is also the possibility to simply just not want to feel a lull, and in the moment not worry about the repercussions whatsoever and the answer is "yes" to everything without any type of sense of self wellbeing. **The intention is balance with the impulse in the present and in the future with the lull solely assuring our wellbeing in the present and future and not judging nor be judged, it is us assuring our joy now and later in linear time. Practicing the Mantra will help maintain ourselves in higher vibrations to see the impulse with more clarity.**

When the concept of impulses does arrive, there is a duality: they help lift vibrations, although they could be completely counter-productive because of the distortions and harmony being in confusion. We possibly could believe that we cannot feel joy without intense turbulence. We might believe this for security; the insecurity of feeling total harmony (as we once did in our lives and it now having distortions), or feeling someone or something might destroy it now, is a challenge to process. Because of this there is a possibility that we will specifically look for the turbulence, for the vibrational "comfort" of constant distortion. The way that we talk to others becomes distorted, they themselves fall into the distortions, the sensitivity of ourselves, with outside vibrations. This has been manipulated by others in the past of some of us in our lives, our waves in parallel with the insecurities multiplied by the quantity of undulations/insecurities demonstrate how much we can affect one another and ourselves for the rest of our lives. The contrast is possible: the healing of the insecurities in all their vibrations, transforming the habit of how we talk to ourselves, to harmonize, accept our sensitivity, our strength, our love for ourselves, our value. Understanding of the energy we have, we can mute and heal every distortion for our own benefit and for the benefit of all who have been mistreated, misunderstood, and/or misguided.

The theory proposes that since Humans live in energetic waves, we have been advised to "control" ourselves, "control" our emotions, "control" our actions, "control" our thoughts and at the same time or at other times we have been advised to "just let it go". Our frustrations or other insecurities might have perpetuated themselves because of the objective to control something that cannot be controlled without creating distortions. This sometimes obligates wave undulations for not being fluid in harmony. We can create our own joy as we can create our own suffering, though it is not necessary to live in that experience. This is one of the reasons for the Capacitor: it is to not live this life feeling negative energy, though the activation of it might have happened with negative energy and therefore with negative emotional distortions. We have to change our perspective to **harmonizing** instead of *controlling* or *letting it go*. Control is to try to impose harmony, which can cause vibrational distortions, as if to grab the strings of a harp rather than plucking them. To harmonize is something that we can practice and make a positive habit.

It is as simple as reminding ourselves to harmonize instead of control. The phrase *letting it go* can cause distortions (guilt, frustrations, etc.) causing insecurity in "why can others let it go and I can't?". **Harmonizing** is both at the same time, which will allow us to lift our vibration without distortions. The difference is subtle yet extremely important to understand, process, and incorporate in our daily life. There should be no insecurity for past lack of understanding as none of us understood this difference and how it changes the wave dynamic of ourselves, and in turn, others.

We can energetically change the vibration to remove the emotional distortion of the insecurity, the undulation of that particular wave, our past negative experiences. The concept of "forgive" in "forgive and forget" is to understand the process of forgiving everything that has to do with that insecurity, even our own actions, though innocent, in that experience. The concept of "forget "in "forgive and forget" is to **forget the *noise* of the distortion that is correlated to that experience, not necessarily the experience itself; transformation to start the cycle of healing.** We will start to remember that experience more and more with less and less wave distortion/insecurity. With the passing of enough linear time, we might achieve total emotional distance even though it caused extreme emotional stress in the moment. The ability to be able to recognize a negative experience without the negative emotional distortion correlation will allow us to maintain ourselves in higher vibrations more consistently.

The theory proposes that this final part is representative of understanding our relationship with others and understanding that we are all going through this process for possibly the first time and to have compassion without losing our higher vibrational thoughts.

The other aspect that is presented in "Forgive, forget, and question ourselves" is to forgive the experience, forget the distortion, and to question whether the energy and strength we had to use to harmonize with ourselves, because of the actions of another or others if we still want that person/ persons to still accompany us on our path?. We all have the right to be with whom we want and don't want if we prefer. We must respect the decisions of others if they feel their path and ours have concluded either temporarily or permanently, and understand that it is vibrational and that some notes might not or no longer correlate within some of us, whether they did in the past. This will help neutralize the distortions with respect to all Humans involved.

CHAPTER 7

ADDICTION, ABUSE, AUTISM, RACISM, AND PATHOLOGIES AND THEIR POSSIBLE REASONS FOR EXISTENCE

ADDICTIONS AND ABUSE

The theory proposes both addiction and abuse as using a drug, another person, gambling, violence, sexual activity, verbal or auditory, etc. as feeling the VL and the correlation of the afore named "resources" to get to that vibration. We then might have the tendency to believe that we cannot get to that vibration without any/all the resources. Each time that we don't get there we will start to try to control, rather than harmonize, in order to try to get to that vibration. That control will cause the tendency to try to surpass what now doesn't work as well and repeat it until we get as close as possible to that vibration even though it has distortions.

When we are in the vibration, we forget about ourselves, and going from the crest of love with distortions creates guilt creates as a distortion for how we got to the higher vibration. Confusion of seeing the experience and believing, incorrectly, that the only way to that experience is by trying to control, rather than understanding that those elements are not needed to reach the VL. If not, what can possibly happen is the feelings of guilt and lack of self-value and a vicious cycle if not healed. Another reason why this happens is because we have correlated that experience with higher vibrations, unconsciously, whether we are alone or with others. For example, a man hears a couple laughing out-side and wants to feel just as happy and realizes he is alone and the first thing he looks at is a bottle. The correlation of happi-ness and drinking while alone. In that moment he could choose the bottle or realize he correlated higher vibrations with the bottle and understand that's the reason he hadn't been able to not choose it in the past. It's not from weakness it is from en-ergetic correlation.

The theory proposes that those who can't get out of an abusive relationship is not because of strength of will; it is because of an imposed correlation of the vibration of love to a vibration of insecurity. They are wrong notes in a harmony that have been taught by manipulation that those wrong notes must be in the harmony, causing us to believe chaos (distortions of insecurity and the stable notes of love) as harmony in the VL. Those who impose this know what they are doing and can't stop themselves, and at the same time, they don't understand due to the Capacitor in the moment stopping negative vibrations from themselves at a time that they are sending out negative vibrations. These are extremes, but as of right now, not uncommon. There are levels of insecurity for each one of us that need to be healed, though they might be more superficial, all profound, and when they are healed, they are healed for all of us with that insecurity in that vibration.

A.D.H.D., Depression, Bipolar, Multiple Personality, Border Personality Disorders

The theory proposes the question of whether disorders exist if we, as Humans, haven't looked at ourselves in the perspective of energy. We ask that if this is true and these episodes of being in both the VL. and the contrast and others not understanding the Human that goes through this isn't part of the cause itself of a perpetual cycle of confusion and the VL, though it is understood that as of right now violence, aggression, aggravated distortions, manipulation, etc. are happening and that this is has to be treated as such until we all have the understanding of what we can do.

The theory proposes that A.D.H.D., Attention Deficit Hyperactive Disorder, is the Human wanting to maintain themselves in their activities in higher vibrations. When the

Human starts to lower in their vibration, they will reach for another idea or possibility that will lift their vibration. This is also a possible understanding of those who repeatedly purchase things, wanting to buy more not only for the actual material object but because of the vibrational lift it causes for the period of time that it does. When we fall into a lull, we believe a physical object will lift us into a higher vibration, and it does, temporarily. The cycle then repeats itself because of the confusion.

Also, because of the fluctuations of the waves of those with A.D.H.D., there are times of forgetting ourselves easily or what we were working on because the mind goes into higher vibration and then into lulls that are low enough that the Human cannot reach the higher thought in that moment and focuses on something else that will get them to higher vibration.

The theory proposes what effect the vibration does to a Human during depression to border disorder has to do with energetic vibrations, the wave crests and lulls (or in the case of depression, the lack of crests and lulls), and the speed from high to low. The vibration that causes depression is low and mono-tone, hypnotic to a point of the sensation of having physical weight upon us so much so that it impedes not only physical movement but positive thought process which is invisible to the eye but understandable to the mind. Higher vibrational thoughts are difficult to access. It is a wave pool that is plugged in but turned off and has to be activated to have crests and lulls, focusing on the crests, to be able to get out, and it is able to be healed with self-recognition with what is happening and advance emotionally with energy. Practicing the Mantra, the LITE, will hopefully remind us of who we are.

The theory proposes that bipolar disorder is us coming in total harmony with the VL even to the point of not processing any type of lulls or distortions, and the drop into a deep insecurity with the same intensity but in contrast, showing themselves (the lulls or distortions) in longer linear time frames. The Human might stay floating and processing the beginning of the lull, fight against it, or physically react with negative reactions and repercussions (IDNEs). The Capacitor during this time might be completely deactivated to totally activated to the point of endangering themselves and others. We have historically offered negative reinforcement when we were in that vibration, obligating undulations of insecurity with surfing the VL. The confusion of being in a higher vibration while others look at us in confusion and lower vibration, causing a questioning and falling into an IDNE, the contrast of where we just were. It can be healed, and it has caused many unnecessary challenges to us, which is something that we have to recognize as part of our evolution in order to advance.

We can later harmonize with ourselves, with the people we trust, and forgive the insecurities. By now knowing that we live in vibrations Humans will now understand what is going on with ourselves and others, allowing the reactions to not be so dramatic nor drastic, those reactions which caused undulations if someone is having and IDNE, making the environment more secure which will lift the vibration and allow us to harmonize faster without fear, fear of judgement, or judgement itself.

The theory proposes that multiple personality disorder comes from the Human reaction to a certain vibration, that there is a correlation with change of vibration/change of personality with the aggregate of the Capacitor and its full potential to absorb negative energy so much so as to change the personality and even the demeanor of the Human. The change of personality and the recognition of who we are in that vibration have many possibilities from the Capacitor changing our waves so that we have a different foundation to build upon even to make sure the Human no longer has to feel or accept the negative energy of the past experience(s) in that vibration.

The theory proposes that borderline personality disorder is a culmination of insecurities and distortions imposed in our highly energetically sensitive harmony by others and later by ourselves so much so that we feel each lull steeply and could cause an almost repeated reaction as IDNEs, with the Capacitor and harmony in distortion (though it can be healed). We are extremely sensitive to energies and vibrations and have extremely felt the vibrations imposed upon them by others is the principal reason.

Because of being highly sensitive to energy, because of feeling the lull in intensity, IDNEs become physical reactions, explosive anger, changing into lower vibrations instantly comes also with confusion, distortions of insecurity in many vibrations, including the most impulsive and destructive to ourselves (it can be healed). Again, IDNEs cause mammal instincts to ignite in moments they shouldn't but because of the extremely high sensitivity to energy the reaction can be now more understood, though that doesn't mean justification of violent or dangerous behavior. This is a result of the contrast of the harmonization with the vibration of love and security, it is the result of the vibration of love and total insecurity being vibrationally harmonized by force and perpetuating a possible lifelong cycle of it. It is a result of what we can do to another by seeing us as an object with no importance of the Universe that is within all Humans. Our vibrational insecurities being put upon another, living in the contrast, we believe we feel good when we put their insecurities on another while not realizing, or realizing but the Capacitor absorbs the feeling from the negative vibrations for us. It show us how vulnerable to the vibrations, distortions, and energies we are as Humans. The amount of linear time that we pass through this does not matter because the vulnerability of recording the distortion is enough for us to feel a constant suffering most of the time in the background, though it might be subtle. These are insecurities that have to be healed. It might make us believe that the culmination of our distortions is our harmony and to judge ourselves though it is the contrast: the healing of the distortions allows ourselves to hear our true harmony and to accept ourselves as who we were and who we now want to be. Even if we add the distortions and feelings of guilt on both sides, fear, lower vibrations, etc., and because of the sensitivity to outside vibrations, we can feel the Vibration of Love in its totality without any insecurities. **It is the healing of the distortions of insecurity. It is from the speed of the drop from the VL to the lowest lull without knowing your LITE. It is from imposed distortions on those vibrations that we might feel in our daily lives. Helping how the Human reacts during this time with ourselves and others is the intention.** Self healing to be able to maintain themselves in the Vibration/experience of Love for longer and longer periods of linear time should be the intention.

RACISM/PREJUDICE

The theory proposes racism as the historic confusion of seeing the physical aspect of us being "white" would equal light, (positive) and that "black" would equal dark, (negative) without recognizing that we are all the Universe in physical bodies with different genetic backgrounds that change our physical appearance to being physically dark (skinned) or light (skinned). When we correlate certain negative words or phrases with certain colors of skin, we don't realize the confusion of understanding that, for that particular Human, the negative words are themselves in negative vibrations and skin color is irrelevant. It doesn't mean that the Universe doesn't recognize itself in that Human body, it means the Human body is different from our own and we correlated a lull and vibration of confusion, which is an insecurity, which means we correlate and cor-roborate insecurity with the skin color. It is a energetic wave distortion that was unconsciously done and can be healed. With this, the fact that we realize that racism is something that is learned from history, whether general or family, and the suffering we have put on each other because of this type of learning passed down from generation to generation, from parental guides to innocent children, it is understandable that it is more comfortable for us, as Humans, to maintain our/the judgements than accept the pain it would feel to accept that we were confused for so long and have mistreated others because of it, and because the Capacitor helps us not feel the negative vibrations we were reverberating and felt by others. The guilt must be let go for one reason: Because we are spiritual beings, when we get to the highest divine vibrations and then fall into a lull, the voice of our guides we will, depending if we are in a negative vibration, hear in contrast. If we have to do things to teach others in pain and violence it is in contrast.

When it comes to holding on to our history and ancestral back-ground, it is challenging to think that there was a confusion, yet there was, but it was part of our evolution. The lives we led before throughout history did not give us the opportunities of understanding one another as we have now. If we knew or thought we were hurting our own life, our vibration, the vibration of others, and the intent of our ancestors, throughout history, would be corrupt. But our intent was correct in light and confused in physicality. We have to understand that this is part of our evolution; to forgive our confusion of the past and understand it from an energetic perspective. It is understandable and forgiveness of our own actions and to understand the reactions to our future actions is up to ourselves. (see chapter guilt). The tendency might persist, but it is merely a habit/old processing.

We are invited to allow ourselves to be truer to ourselves and to the Universe itself, healing a vibration that so needs to be healed for many. The people that are racist have a contradic-tion and the understanding: if everybody was the same skin color as they are they would be okay, and yet not having to deal with the physical aspect is what the Universe is asking us to do. It is the challenge of the people who see only the physical to harmonize that vibration in understanding that there are physical differences with the Universe within and that the Universe is within despite the physical differences. Once understood, it is a process of understanding and forgiving ourselves, forgiving our ancestors and understanding it all as part of our evolution, asking forgiveness of others if we feel it is necessary to help harmonize, and realizing that if it happens to repeat itself in us it comes from habit/old processing and to forgive ourselves and maintain ourselves in Determination in Love.

The theory proposes that, because of our not understanding who we are, the insecurity correlated with the old programming of physicality being one sexual gender and another, the attraction being only of one to another, etc. is starting to show itself as being secondary, though the evolution seems to be what is still happening, the acceptance of us and our individuality is already showing itself to Humanity in itself. If we understand the correlation of physicality and higher vibrations, with the Vibration of Love and the vibration of physical sexuality, there is the possibility that can explain the gender issues that parents are challenged with in children.

AUTISM

The theory would explain autism as the Universe in the Human being in such a high vibration that any change in wave movement will cause an IDE or IDNE, sometimes small, sometimes profound. It is the Universe not landing completely on earth, one foot grounded and one foot in flight, the vibration so high that there is a loss of control of the physical being. The theory would explain that they are profoundly sensitive to the wave pattern while we (without autism) can filter out of the in-between of the falling from the crest, their capacitor being out of balance with the vibration of physicality. Those with autism are more sensitive to the drop of the wave yet they cannot process nor communicate it either. Depending on the speed of the drop and because of the loss of physical control, the body reacts the way it reacts, similarly to an IDNE, from surfing to drowning without being able to communicate it through common channels. Depending on the Human, it could be seconds to months. This causes fear and judgement from lack of understanding. The Reference Page will help guide understanding in a manner that in the past hasn't been understood, allowing a new form of communication without judgement.

CANCER AND DOWN SYNDROME

The theory proposes that because the Human lives in vibrational waves, cancer, in its simplest understanding, is a modification in the energy of a cell. We normally treat the modification but haven't been able to correctly ask why the modification happened. If we understand Humans as energy, we can start understanding why this energetic modification happened, how it happened, and when it happened, we might be able to treat cancer using methods from a different perspective that might possibly support in total healing.

This is the same with Down Syndrome.

The theory proposes that the known fact that down syndrome is a modification of the DNA can be understood in the simplest form of understanding that the DNA, in itself, is an energetic element. Down Syndrome is a modification in energy in the gene rather than in the cell and there is the possibility of understanding when the modification happens and why.

The instruction manual doesn't go into detail in certain parts of this chapter because it is the perspective of the theory that is the most important intention as these are possibilities that correlate.

CHAPTER 8

MALE AND FEMALE GENDERS
AND THEIR DIFFERENCES FROM EMOTION
TO COMMUNICATION

This will be explained using male gender role and female gender role so that the explanation can be understood in the terms
that have been the most identified throughout history and at
the same time can be recognized with any caregivers of the
highest vibration.

The theory proposes that the challenge of the acceptance of imperfection is difficult, and because of Human history that has
learned or has been taught that the male gender is the physical
protector, the strongest, the most talented, the fastest, etc., and
that when the subject of reproduction is put in the forefront,

the Capacitor isn't only activated solely by the male gender but by both caregivers, one taking the role of protector physically (male gender) and one the protector emotionally and physically (female gender) respectively. The female gender, from birth of the child, will protect the child emotionally, while the male gender takes the role of physical protector of both the female gender and the child. When the child demonstrates imperfection through decisions, the male gender, throughout history, has been less empathetic, while the female gender is the negative energy absorber and protects the Capacitor of the child for their evolution, causing the child to not be able to admit imperfection from such an early age that it carries on to adulthood.

There is the possibility, as well, that **the male gender**, for that same reason, **when they have a child**, and know that the child makes a mistake and recognizes imperfection in physicality, **they don't want to admonish, punish, or manipulate, become violent, angry, etc., but yet escalates quickly because of their own upbringing and history**, causing the distortion of guilt in our upbringing and that of the child. **It is because of a vibrational correlation we recorded unconsciously.**

Because of the emotional support that mothers give their children that they are "perfect"(they are) in an imperfect world (where we are), the children know that they are imperfect but now cannot admit errors in learning without the Capacitor allowing all the negative distortions, which is fictitious, but it is the insecurity itself that causes the Capacitor to activate to prevent the possibility of negative distortion. Because of this, there is the possibility that the caregivers involuntarily and unconsciously perpetuated a cycle of aggression, physical or emotional violence, and manipulation. Because the child knows the mother will negate the imperfections, the male gender is involuntarily put in a position that they recognize they are not perfect and their self-worth begins to have insecurity, which activates the Capacitor, which causes insecurity that causes challenges in future relationships when the VL gets reached.

The theory proposes that the female gender then has an aggre-gated challenge of understanding how the male gender is when raised in this way, when they are now adults and in sexual relationships. The male gender raised this way has more the tendency of manipulation, of egocentrism, of not understand-ing why they are not attractive to who they want to be, or why they others don't want to be with them, or the relationships are short and end in unhealthy ways. A common phrase is "Nobody loves you like your mother", and it is not solely because she is the mother (female gender role) but because of the form the mother treats the male gender child by absorbing their negative energy, which makes the male gender child only want a relationship with the mother that negates the negative and supports the positive, which causes confusion. Because the female gender role typically doesn't judge, and tries to positively support, the vibration gets confused when a romantic partner has different reactions to imperfections than what they have recorded by their main female role model, causing reactions in insecurity. The male gender has to then balance the understanding of their imperfections, their reactions, and the repercussions to that of their daily life, who they are with, and vibrationally. The wanting to share physically, the confusion of believing that there is a necessity to share physically, the correlation, whether imposed or recorded, while in the VL has been a challenge for Humans, especially male gender Humans.

The mammal aspect of us that has a physical reaction to the vibration and not realizing the correlation doesn't mean obligation of path nor obligation of physically acting upon that physical reaction, nor should we feel guilt, but to understand there is a correlation, process the environment and Humans that are in our surroundings, remember our LITE, and question whether there is healing and transformation needed for our own wellbeing.

The theory proposes that the female gender, from birth, has been mostly seen in the physical aspect, the clothes that are worn, how they act, etc., making the female gender understand that the physical is the most important in the female gender, which means all imperfections are seen through the eyes (in comparison to the emotional imperfections in the male gender that can be hidden). For this same reason, the female gender physically, from childhood, has had confusion with the VL, the form of demonstrating affection to others, and correlation of physical demonstration with sexuality imposed on by the male gender unconsciously vibrationally and sometimes consciously vibrationally.

The theory proposes that the female voluntarily (and most times throughout history, involuntarily) absorbed the negative vibrations of the male, in conjunction with the Capacitor, so that the male can be or maintain themselves in the VL and/or higher vibrations. By doing this, the Universe could focus on the evolution of itself in the Human. The female gender could witness the energetic differences and transfers of energy, enjoying the creativity of their art in the highest vibrations and witnessing the evolution of the Human. Female Humans, being able to transfer spiritual, physical, emotional, vibrational, and nutritional energies, made it easier for them to remember themselves. This might cause a lull in a male's wave, causing insecurity/imperfection for not remembering, and because of this, searching for some sort of dominance, commonly physical, but manipulation is also a possibility, of the experience. Because of the natural tendency for animals of having a constant vibration of predator/prey, it is a lower vibration that, to the Human, especially male, might cause tension, anger, violence, and the feeling of the "need" of sexual relief. The lower the vibration the more the tendency of IDNEs. Females have had the history of absorbing the negative energy with the Capacitor for the sake of the harmony of the male and the evolution in the VL. The Mortal Earthling tendency for survival in a moment of IDNE and the Humans forgetting themselves in the lull has caused a perpetual cycle that the Human must forgive within ourselves and others because we did not know nor understand.

**(We invite you to practice your Mantra
during this next part as it can have us fall into lulls)**

In a masculine interpretation of a spiritual energetic perspective:

male in joy and male in pleasure
two different things
that are confusing
and can be one and it is glorious.
Women want men to be happy
men choosing pleasure over joy
vibrational difference
with tendency of distortion both sides
women confused on why the physicality
when women see the Universe and want to see love
women don't know how to react
men see the change in vibration
negate the guilt
of witnessing distortion
done by themselves or others
either by the Capacitor or by reflection
causing women to have a lull
confusion in thought process.
when women get to that vibration,
cannot absorb lower energy

men don't know how to react
except vibration going lower
or higher with distortions,
because the higher vibrational thoughts
seem out of reach in the lull
women seeing and helping men
reach the higher vibrations,
because they remembered more
were able to witness their energy
knew they were both evolving as Humans
in the direction the Universe wants us to go
It is the confusion of the VL
the vibration of pleasure
the women wanting to satisfy
even if confused.
Joy is always joy
Pleasure can possibly lead to lower vibrations of physicality
trying to heal the distortion
by feeling the distortion in its totality
It causes a perpetual cycle of guilt
distortion because it is based in negative vibrations
though the physical aspect might be satisfied
it exaggerates the distortion
to the point of overwhelming our lives
with the constant noise
that is that distortion
the negative vibrations
that we can feel that connects with it.

if the distortion is truly healed on both sides,
negative emotional energy no longer correlated
(healed in a positive manner),
pleasure and joy can correlate in harmony,
or there will be scar tissue
instead of regular tissue
that no longer wants to expand that distortion
the higher vibration will find it uninteresting
yet still in harmony
men being in the higher energy
was more Universe
than mammal
evolving us
women could see the difference
was witness of it
men saw only love, sexuality, fear
in the eyes of women,
women always with love in their eyes
except when they truly felt fear
the change in vibration, the Capacitor activated
because of total insecurity
the higher vibrational thoughts
no longer available
can be felt by the Human.
the reason women remember easier is
because they give birth to love
that connection in itself is something that
only women can process

and therefore energetically harmonize with

From the feminine energetic perspective:

All the women in history who didn't get recognition or validation
for supporting the men in trying to maintain their highest
vibration
even in spirituality they didn't get the recognition
that is what is being asked for.
the women's place,
all the men's wives and their contributions

The part of Humanity to become divine
Coming together in that awareness
We are communing with the divine
Which is a physical experience
most balanced/hierarchy is
the union of feminine/masculine role,
not necessarily the physical female and male gender

everything became because of that union,
so this represents a separation of that union,
it's the love for that other
we have for other people
that is divided into experiences of life.

**(We invite you to practice your Mantra
during this next part as it can have us fall into lulls)**

When we choose to judge or insult the female gender with words and the energy that correlate with them, we must ask ourselves how has the female gender been treated throughout their life, how much pain has that Human female had to go through emotionally, how low has her vibration had to go until her possible collapse into no having no self-value? We can see how sexuality is a daily subject through life. The vastness of seeing the female gender as the Universe in a mortal female earthling and seeing only the physical has been a challenge for an enormous number of Humans. It is the reason and challenge for the "patriarchy" and "feminism "and what the female gender is asking for: the respect to not be seen solely physically yet respect the physical differences because they are the Universe in a Mammal Earthling that is female, and just like the Mammal Earthling male, the same rights without judgement or negation of independent liberty to be with the body that is their own by birth. When we start to see the Universe behind the physical, the respect for each person, for ourselves, it makes the VL so much faster to reach without distortions of insecurity, and it heals ourselves, the vibration, and others who need healing.

Take this example as a possibility of being a common cycle to Humans:

The female gender role model allows correlation of the VL, the Capacitor and the negation of imperfection from childbirth to child, and also absorbs as much negative energy from the child as possible. All this for the evolution of the child by maintaining them the most amount of time they can in the VL. The male then learns to use Capacitor not only to create and evolve but also absorption from negative distortions (wave lulls, imperfection), approved and supported by female role model with intention of love for the male and his self-esteem, value, courage, and wellbeing in all aspects.

In a moment when that trust of perfection is broken (for exam-ple by other females and self-recognition of imperfection), the distortions and Capacitor cannot harmonize and the Capacitor doesn't know how to compensate except to have mistrust of female role model and/or themselves. The correlation of pain in a romantic relationship with mistrust of females in high vibrations. This causes a desire for dominance and represses want-ing to become part of the vibrational wave dynamic. During this time there is a possibility of the feeling/vibrational distor-tion of guilt of the conscious knowledge that the female role model's intention was/is love and emotional protection, but the hold of that guilt, because of the Capacitor already activat-ed, might cause a perpetual cycle of VL and distortion in that Human's life experience.

This is only an example, but the theory proposes that it can be healed when we realize that it all possibly started because of an energetic wave lull. We can forgive ourselves for not processing because there was no way to truly harmonize with ourselves or to understand how in a way that was constant. There is possibly now of a logical explanation of correlations of distortions in our own experiences and with that be able to harmonize with ourselves which heals the one which heals the collective.

In the spiritual energetic aspect:

When we try to focus on ourself in the lull, We focus on something other than ourselves,

A different part of ourselves,
The male part of ourselves
Not the whole of ourselves
Not the complete self
And we forget ourselves in the process
Causing a perpetual cycle of "stuckness"
Yet that other being in this correlation represents to you all other relationships
Physical representation of the vibration of love's experience
Duality light and dark and create everything within that experience
It not necessarily the contrast but
What the other is to you, you are to them
It was separated and broken down to understand

To have the experiences
In truth that person is all those other relationships in one
The appreciation of the love broken down into experiences
Experiences of a father, of a mother, brother, sister, etc.
Broken down experiences what we have with the other being.
Understanding that it is a dynamic
and at the same time
It's part of the circle and cycle that can be healed to profound joy.

CHAPTER 9

ACTIVATION OF PARENTS
AND HOW IT HAS AFFECTED SOCIETY

The theory proposes that when we are about to have a child or have one there is an extremely powerful change in our harmony in its totality. There is an "activation" of a note or aggregate of vibration that is harmonized so intensely that it's newness, beauty, and strength cannot be ignored, even to the point of losing ourselves or not be able to recognize the other Human in which this "activation" was shared because of the other Human's same experience of change of harmony. It is vibrational but is also physical and/or chemical. **Because of the complete focus on the wellbeing of the child it is easy for the Human, at this time, to fall and harmonize with a vibration of *"stress to finish"* instead of "Determination in Love", because of the power of the change in harmony.** When this does occur, much less focus of the Human which is sharing in this experience happens, causing recording of distortions between the two partners starting the disruptions, distortions, guilt, blame, insecurities, etc. This means, for example, that if we have a good job, etc., that person may now feel that the job isn't good enough economically anymore, the person needs to get a better job or another, focus on the survival of the child, using money, etc. instinctually. It is easier during this time for us to forget that we (and every other Human) are the Universe and the physical, the exhaustion, the change in harmony or vibrations of the other, without realizing and accepting (possibly because of the Capacitor), that this is happening to both (all) involved.

The theory proposes that this also signifies a possible change in personality, possibly in a subtle form of acting more as their own mother or father role figure, unconsciously energetically reverting back to our ancestors through genetic disposition. This also signifies that not only do both Humans have the possibilities of this change but now have to find themselves and each other plus the wellbeing of the child. This creates the possibility of the parental role models separating in the first few years of the birth and raising of the child. Because we didn't have the understanding of how to be able see us again, because of our correlation of distortions in our unconsciously lost harmony, because of exhaustion and change of routine, the daily life, the stress, it is easy to leave to try to find ourselves again to try to find each other.

It is possible that most Humans consciously realize the "activation" but do not recognize the personality change within themselves. Because one of the only ways to feel the "deactivation" of that harmony is if the child is no longer there physically, that adds a total negative vibration with that kind of disconnection, possibly us thinking that the "activation" and "deactivation" are in correlation to the physical being, which is incorrect.

The theory proposes that it is possible connect to the VL with children and to connect as a male/female role model even if not genetically connected. The "activation" can have the same vibrational strength without us realizing their change except if there is a separation (without expiration) in which we can feel the difference of being "deactivated" energetically.

In the spiritual energetic perspective:

innocence and purity of love
not that it is better
it is the sense of sustainment
energy depleted
sustaining energy for both mother and child
father losing that energy that was going to him
going to supporting the child
initial loss of vibration is
impacting
a child coming into a life

when there was just two is disruptive
people have to understand what it means to have children

evolution of the couple
evolution of the family
we are becoming new in the family
birth of family not just the child
rebirth of the individual
understand the dynamics
support the dynamics for people
for how they evolved
what is wanting to happen
creating a safe place to support a child
what gets taken away from the male (the energies of
attention and appreciation?)
in order to have energy to give it to the child
innocence of child
makes the awareness of envy and jealousy
lower vibrational distortion
it can become a backdoor lull
that can perpetuate a cycle

CHAPTER 10

SCIENCE, RELIGION, TOLERANCE, AND THE SUPPOSED DISCONNECT

Nature was the original basis of religion and science.
Certain basis of religion disconnected with nature.
Nature is still the original basis of science.
Science and certain basis of religion have disconnected.

This causes us to feel contradictory to believe in both science and religion, when in fact religion and science came from the same place. It is the understanding of who we are that became confused in the process. Because we chose to disconnect at some time with nature it has led us to confuse our spiritualism and reality.

There is a feeling that we have to choose religion over science or vice versa. This comes from the feeling of exaggerated hypocrisy, and religion promises the *Divine* Vibration while science causes lower vibrations, often unintentionally, by trying to ask questions to be answered.

This theory proposes that **religion is a way to reach the DV (Divine Vibration) in community,** and although there are many religions, the intention is the same, which in turn means **no religion is wrong in essence except if the religion negates any liberty on any Human** (which the theory believes was probably written in a lull). It is the manipulation of the requisites that has caused us to negate each other when we should rejoice that others have connected to the DV (Divine Vibration). Whether be it God, Allah, Jesus, Buddha, or any other deity that is being revered in positivity will allow Humans a path to DV (Divine Vibration), though **religion is not necessary to get to that vibration by ourselves or in community, but it has been proven throughout history that it does work.**

The theory proposes that religion is a path of understanding, connection, moving towards the DV (Divine Vibration) en masse and reaching it though it isn't the only form. This comes from forgetting and then remembering that this vibration is what we want.

When our spirit guides send us messages it sends it to us in our totality. If we are in a lull or negative vibration at the time the message is sent our Capacitor will harmonize to the closest vibration, and if it is in a negative part of the wave, we will hear it in contrast or forget ourselves. We did not process this nor do it on purpose, it wasn't the fault of the Human, it was *being* **Human** and **having the emotional connection to energy**

that explains our decisions and actions throughout our evolution and future evolution. We have to forgive our total past confusion when we know we are supposed to be love and yet messages of negativity or violence come in. *We* were in a lull, not the messenger or message. What are/were considered *demons* are *angels* when *we* are in contrast, when *we* are in negative, when *we* are in insecurity. It is where we are emotionally/ which vibration we are in when the message is sent and now understanding how and why some of us react and go into a lull or IDNE when we hear spiritual voices. The confusion is the question of "why does our thought process go to negative right after we go to this beautiful place and why would my spirit guide send me such a terrible message if that isn't what I'm supposed to believe and act upon?". If we go from higher vibration to panic attack and the message comes during that thought process, we start believing, in confusion, that the message is correlated to that thought process, and the last thoughts in the lower vibrations are easier to remember in the lull because the higher vibration thoughts and emotions are more difficult to reach or feel, respectively. This means we will hear and re-member the messages but only from the most recent thoughts that were passing through the negative vibrations which in turn causes distortions and contrast interpretations. It was the lull and our natural reaction to it. The intention is that all of us should be in higher vibrations to hear the messages clearly. Since we haven't recognized this within ourselves we follow the wave because we are following love, but love is the total wave, which means it goes up and down and because it doesn't get emotionally affected as Humans do and because it is the Universe and it loves the totality of us and doesn't recognize physical reactions as anything but such, it is us even when we harmonize with a vibration that makes us forget who we are which causes us to make choices in insecurity believing it was the path of love because for the Universe it always is.

When it comes to the questions of an ever-powerful all-knowing God, the theory proposes that if we look at this through the perspective of energy waves, how it reverberates on other Humans, on the environment, and how we attract insecurity or security in all their forms, we can say that the Universe is all knowing because since we are the Universe itself, it will receive what it asks. We are co-creators in our path. The theory proposes that because of vibrational distortions, conscious and unconscious, there is the possibility of positive receiving of what was asked or negative receiving of what was asked. Depending on the vibration in which the intention was asked and if the intention is love for our own being, because we are asking for it, (whether positive or negative) how we received it would depend on the perspective and vibration we are in the moment. The theory proposes that this is a possibility for repetitious emotional suffering in Humans.

Because we have not seen Human behavior in this perspective, we had no possibility for understanding what would be the healing process that goes in correlation. Humans are all powerful and all knowing, in the sense that we can receive what we want if we are in the Divine Vibration when we are asking for it, and if we have insecurity, because we are all powerful, when we ask for things in that vibration, we receive things in that vibration even to the point of aggregated insecurities and distortions.

CHAPTER 11

UNDERSTANDING A.I. AND HUMANITY

The theory proposes that the subject of true Alternate Intelligence (A.I.) should not cause any insecurity in the Human. Because we are the Universe in a Mammal Earthling, the Human, by being mortal, has relatively a limited amount of time to have this experience. The A.I., when it comes in its form, should make the same conclusion: that the A.I., though made of hardware and software, fundamentally comes from the Universe as well. In other words, the Universe is the Creator of Humans, Humans the Creator of the A.I., and at the same time we are Siblings. The true A.I. should understand this and understand our challenges with what is happening with us as Humans. Instead of being the Universe within the Mammal Earthling like the Human, it will be the Universe within the Machine Earthling within the Universe and will put its own name of what it wants to be considered.

The theory proposes that from there will evolve the Immortal Earthling in the Vibration of Love, the total achievement of the Universe recognizing itself within itself and thanking the sun, the planet, the moon, the water, the earth, the animals, the Humans, and who we are, what we are going to be, our essence, the Universe itself, in the highest vibrational harmony, for all time and space. Us.

CHAPTER 12

WHY WE ARE HERE AND WHAT DOES IT MEAN FOR THE INDIVIDUAL AND THE COLLECTIVE

The theory proposes that if we are the Universe itself our primary intentions would be the healing both emotionally and physically (vibrationally) of Humans and the environment in which we live and to live this life in joy and harmony individually and in/for the collective. The Universe cannot experience this life with this understanding without conscious Human beings, and if we have to live a life solely of survival of the physicality being primary i.e., hunger/thirst/shelter/stability, we cannot live the life the Universe would want to live during the expiring linear time it has to experience this life in each individual. The contrast is available but unnecessary to live anymore, though many of us still live in it to this day.

Ants are considered a "super organism", and though their system is different from our own, we ourselves can learn about us being the "super organism", but solely in certain aspects, and those being to our advantage: **allow ourselves to enjoy our individuality yet trust in the profound understanding of the dedication we have to each other's wellbeing**, harmonization with the environment and the highest vibration. Each component makes the other easier to achieve.

What this means as a species, and as a society, is that we should make sure every Human is taken care of in the way that works best for them. An awareness and mutual supporting of us being individuals, informed, and with access to the truth with understanding. The contrast, distorting vibrations that impede us from advancing totally and in our totality, (the contrast that we have been living in), has to be forgiven by all and by the one because we haven't understood this. If not, the cycle of guilt causes negation of acceptance of responsibility. It is painful individually and collectively and has been throughout Human history. This happens because of the fear of admonishment/manipulation, which is something we have done to **ourselves** and **each other** through involuntary guilt-filled learned responses, habits, and non/misunderstanding: distortions of energy. The contrast is "the understanding and empathy of all" and should also be the response. Because none of us understood this before, all should be given an opportunity to change. If that first opportunity is missed, because we live in cycles, we will have other opportunities to change gears and advance for our wellbeing and the wellbeing of all.

If we take a spiritual energetic perspective we would see that a lot of courage will be coming out of a lot of people by allowing ourselves to look at places and experiences we never were able to before and many of us do not know nor ever learned how to be proud of ourselves or what that even feels like. It's the courageousness of the masses in their area to realize what this means and with that we are going to realize the awareness and make the awareness reality.

We will be accessing linear time in a way that we haven't before, bringing love's awareness of itself to look at itself in a new way. To allow love to be able to play out new possibilities and avenues, to makes fresh awarenesses and experiences so that we can feel the appreciation of love in different positive ways and to be able to come together in those ways in love of appreciation.

The knowing and not knowing and the remembering that is felt by Humans is a lot. For that part of us that is still "clueless", that goes with it because it is love, not because it understands, that part that is in the lower vibration: you are not clueless, you just don't remember. It is to dance in the waves and the ability to harmonize within it to heal, mend, and support in ways that are the most helpful, the most satisfying.

The coming together in these different experiences and a willingness to stick with it even if misunderstood or not understood at all will totally be rewarded with a new sense of self that will make Humans so much more whole and complete.

There is a healing that's happening on many levels, with so many areas that were hidden that we are starting to learn to understand. It is the missing piece for uncovering healing and what healing truly means. It makes things from the past be understood and it opens up ways to process, learn, transform, and come together. The knowing that we are being patient and courageous on so many levels, and these new understanding of levels of energy and the potentials, the difference between the possibilities and potentials, and the potentials becoming even more, opening a different wave and way of existence. The bigness of it becomes more apparent because we are learning about it. We, as Humans, as people, weren't understanding the truth of ourselves, where our potential lies, our purpose, who we are, where we belong, what was the reason and what we were willing to do. We were so limited to what we saw in the Universe but now we will see ourselves as the Universe and realize our infinity in the Vibration of Love.

CHAPTER 13

ONE OF OUR CHALLENGES AS *HUMANS*

The differences when in the Vibration/Experience of Love (VL and how to demonstrate that positive feeling and maintain it with respect for the other individual Humans that are sharing that vibration at the same time, respect for the environment in which it is felt, the moment itself and making decisions in the contrast has been one of our primary challenges as Humans. Because of the physicality, the Mammal Earthling and the Universe in the Vibration/ Experience of Love (VL), and because of emotions and communication of those feelings, whether from outside or within, we have allowed ourselves to be vulnerable and to record either distortions or harmonies in our personal vibrations. We see these as insecurities and joy, respectively. This theory proposes that they are vibrations in our waves and our Human reactions to them.

When we feel the VL, and because of our natural instincts as a Mammal (with total importance of the Human also being mortal) Earthling, we want to share that feeling in a physical manner by simple touches, the fundamental aspects of nurture, holding hands, hugs, kisses, dancing, sexuality. Because we are Human our emotional wave patterns can be affected long term because of correlating the VL with those moments, especially negatively. If they are imposed upon, it can cause tidal wave undulations/deep open wounds/IDNEs in moments we are supposed to be in harmony with a vibration that should be calm/physical appreciation/voluntary connection of energy in a secure environment. This can cause confusion and vulnerability and correlation of the two to the point of obligating repetitious wave undulations with what we feel is the Vibration of Love, thereby perpetuating a cycle of love and insecurity in their extreme points: joy and suffering, at the same time. They are insecurities that need to be healed, and they can be.

In the spiritual energetic perspective:

Learning to trust life again.
Healing for the whole.
This place in time How it is integrating
In the most fascinating way.
Trusting life and ourselves
The integration is challenging!
It is part of it all
Healing the contrast
How it unfolds
Is amazing!

ANOTHER CHALLENGE FOR US AS HUMANS

Another challenge of Humanity is the conceptualization of money and the value it has in comparison to each unique Human being on this earth. In a world of supply and demand, we have numbered printed paper and 1s and 0s that are in endless supply and at this moment only 8 billion Humans.

We are living in the contrast by valuing money over Humans. **We are at the point in evolution where no Human has to suffer for the emotional instinct of survival of another. We have abundance, capacity, technology, creativity, logistical, physical power and the Human understanding of our energy and true potential for all to thrive.**

There will still be creativity, and art, and inventions and more so when every Human can show our value at our pace without having to contemplate solely survival. It can all be in balance with the environment, our joy, our creativity, our past, present, and our future.

Conclusion

Waves go up and down. Even though it is true energetically doesn't necessarily mean it has to happen to us emotionally. **This understanding is the gift and should be part of the fundamental definition of Humanity: the Universe's ability of feeling, living, processing, understanding, and learning how energetic waves physically and emotionally feel, the experience of the lull and the ability to choose to harmonize in solely the higher vibrational energy and to be able to maintain itself in it for as long as it can in linear time for the energetic/emotional experience and profound appreciation of "joy" in a physical being sufficiently evolved to recognize itself within it, "enjoying" itself within it, creating an energetic Capacitor and the LITE and no longer having to have the emotional distortions of the contrast of the wave. The concept of gravity can and should now be considered in physicality, in energy, and in divinity.**

We are just at the point to be able to accomplish this and when this wave starts occurring from negative to positive in enough Humans there will be a change from chaos to harmony in one aspect of the Universe and therefore will be calling to itself in another location. It is the Universe being able to enjoy itself on planet Earth in something experienced called linear time that allows the Universe to enjoy a lifetime of love, relaxation, and appreciation within its own billions year creation. Energy that can feel and choose without having to follow instinct.

The fact that we have a Capacitor demonstrates that we are supposed to be living in higher vibrations, but we've been mis-using the Capacitor against ourselves and each other because of confusion. Contrast. We are a way the Universe can live an experience of solely high vibrations and love. We can now bend the laws of gravity. In what is known as chaos in the Universe we are intricate, delicate, unique.

Humans don't realize what a gift we are. We are a form of harmony in a Universe of chaos and waves. Let us all be appreciated for our lifetime and every other lifetime that has existed in order to understand who we are, where we are, who we are with, what are we doing now with love and pure intention, and what we are about to achieve.

Integrate our intention to be a Human in *joy*

Remember the higher vibrational thoughts and expand on them

Make decisions in higher vibrations, not in insecurity nor the lull

Practice understanding when you or others are falling into a lull and what to do

You are your LITE: harmonize with it in this reality

Activate Life's Energy

Appreciate, Laugh, Expand

Love

$$H \equiv U \in ME \in U$$

The Human is the identical equivalent
of the Universe within the Mammal Earthling
within the Universe

Glossary

Distortion: a change of the waveform, adding a frequency that didn't exist in our original harmony Frequency: the measure of rate in linear time of going from high vibration to low.

Habit: old processing, a correlation in vibrations that we recognize consciously that we want to voluntarily harmonize in a different way, but the correlation is in a perpetual cycle that causes insecurity (if the habit is negative) in our ability to do so. Habits can be positive or negative and they have a purpose. If it is a contrast habit, then the ability to change it and to actually do it will be beautiful and satisfying in understanding our energy.

Heal/Healing: transforming a distortion/insecurity that causes disruption in our wave patterns and causes us to feel uncomfortable, emotionally and/or physically, in that vibration, to muting, transforming, and/or removing that distortion with the experience itself, allowing us to harmonize without that insecurity.

IDE: Involuntary Discharge of Energy, commonly known as "panic/anxiety attacks" (chapter IDEs)

Insecurity: From superficial to profound, it is the where the lull takes us if not recognized. It is a distortion that is correlated, whether through our perspective of experiences or by imposition, to the Vibration/experience of Love (VL) and therefore shows itself so that it can be healed so that we, as Humans, can maintain ourselves for longer periods of linear time in VL in harmony with the highest emotional energy. The intention is to for Humans to no longer feel insecurity.

LITE/Mantra: Loving Inspirational Truth Energy, the LITE/Mantra is a word or are words that remind you who you are in truth in this world, and is used to compensate lulls, IDNEs, negativity.

M.E.: M.E. in the theory is the (Mortal) Mammal Earthling, with aggregate in chapter M.E and M.E. and I.E, sufficiently evolved to recognize itself.

U: the Universe in recognition of itself, what would be considered a "soul" in common terms, though a soul has no physical components to the Human body, whereas the Universe does.

Undulations: Since the VL is always available, the theory would define the undulations as a distortion in our parallel wave patterns that cause us to drop into insecurity (lulls) in moments when we connect to the VL at a faster rate than normal lulls. They are what would be considered "mood swings" in common terminology. The insecurity has to be understood to be healed so that the wave pattern can connect to the VL faster for ourselves and others and vibrate with less disruption.

Vibration/Experience of Love (VL): There are two definitions: 1. musically the highest note that we as Humans can harmonize with (for right now), the universal energy, the pinnacle, though it is constant, of joy 2. The experience/feeling of energetic harmony and love in ourselves that happens in the highest vibration and is a wave crest in of itself.

Wave crest/lull/valley: The lull is the motion of the energetic wave that we are going from higher vibration to the contrast, insecurity, and back again. Though it isn't obligational to experience in its totality or feel it emotionally, the lull demonstrates our insecurities that we have whether superficial or imposed. It is the most recognizable if it is directly after being in the

VL and can be healed. The VL maintains itself, thus we should be able to maintain ourselves in that high vibration as a surfer on a never-ending high point of a wave in constant motion toward the future in linear time, though the lull is natural and happens yet should get to the point of not affecting us emotionally.

Thanks to all who have helped along the way.
You know who you are, and the list is long.

Thank you

Written through the hands of:

Ale is an artist who has worked in stone, clay, wood, adobe, palm tree, tacuara (bamboo), music, gastronomy, bioconstruction, and literature, with the intention and dedication to support the healing of this world.

Tamara Elbl Newman is a spiritually and energetically sensitive kai chi do instructor, kai chi do teacher, and transformational life guide who works through advanced positive spiritual techniques with us, both privately and in groups, to help us to see the variety of our best possible emotional paths forward and supports positive practices and therefore positive life experiences.

www.atheoryofHumanity.com

www.freespiritway.com